A PRACTICAL GUIDE TO ACADEMIC RESEARCH

A PRACTICAL GUIDE TO ACADEMIC RESEARCH

Graham Birley
and
Neil Moreland

KOGAN
PAGE

First published in 1998
Reprinted 1999

Kogan Page Limited
120 Pentonville Road
London N1 9JN

British Library Cataloguing in Publication Data

A CIP record for this book is available from the British Library.

ISBN 0 7494 2277 7

Typeset by JS Typesetting, Wellingborough, Northants.
Printed and bound in Great Britain by Biddles Ltd, Guildford and King's Lynn

Contents

Preface 1

1. **Planning a Research Project** 5
Planning the phases of a project
The role of the research question
Sources of research questions
Formulation of research questions
Issues arising from the use of research questions
Periodic review and reflection using research questions
Ethics and research
Gaining access to research sites and data
Developing initial data analysis plans
A word of caution

2. **Obtaining Funding and Access to Conduct Research** 17
Sources of funding
Types of funding
Criteria for the allocation of funds
Making a bid for funding
Construction of a budget for funds
Assessment of project bids
Ethical issues
Supervising and conducting research overseas

3. **Research Methodologies** 28
Theory and originality
Methodology and paradigms
Qualitative and quantitative methodologies
Conclusion: methodologies and some logistical issues

4. **Data Collection** 40
Basic principles of data collection
Planning questionnaires
Planning and conducting interviews
Observation methods

Other forms of data collection
Equipment
Conclusion

5. **The Presentation and Analysis of Data**   58
The three aspects of data analysis
Coding data
Analysing data
Conclusion

6. **Using Literature Sources**   80
Introduction and overview
What does it mean to carry out a review?
Where in a research project is a literature review necessary?
Generic review capabilities
Starting a literature review
Identifying an author's AIMS
Making notes
Comparing and contrasting authors
Writing up your literature review
Using quotations in the text
The presentation of the bibliography
Summary
Looking ahead: Writing up the conclusion

7. **Research and Organizations**   102
Introduction and overview
A definition of an organization
Characteristics of organizations
Perspectives within organizational research and analysis
Possible topics in organizational research
Possible research methods

8. **Quality Improvement and Research in Organizations**   115
Introduction and overview
A definition of quality and its components
Research and identifying and assessing customer needs
Qualitative research approaches and needs identification
Internal process control research
The essence of monitoring and evaluation research
Conclusion

9. **Reflections on the Research Process**   131
    Areas for reflection and meditation in research
    When and how to reflect
    Conclusion

10. **The Computer and Research**   136
    Introduction
    The computer and quantitative data
    The computer and qualitative data
    Getting information via the computer
    The computer and the construction of final research reports
    Other computer uses and sources

11. **Writing the Final Report and Getting the Work Published** 144
    Starting a report
    Originality
    The overall structure of the report
    The completion of the report writing process
    Viva voces of research for higher degrees
    Publishing
    Conclusion

References   155

Further reading   161

Index   163

Preface

All areas of social and educational activity have a research dimension. This is as true of education as it is of history, archaeology or biochemistry. It is still the case, however, that research has difficulties in establishing itself as a root and branch activity in many subjects. Research has to justify its existence far more energetically than do many other activities. Mainly through the sterling work of individuals and of organizations such as the British Educational Research Association (BERA), the American Education Research Association (AERA) and the British and American Sociological Associations, research is making a greater impact upon the lives of practitioners, students, administrators and those benefiting from or purchasing research.

The aim of the present volume is to make further progress in establishing research as a fundamental part of the work of practitioners and organizations concerned to improve the quality of what they do.

This book consequently attempts to meet the needs of all those who are involved in the process of research. Academics and practitioners will find this book of use, but so too will all others who are charged with the job of ensuring quality provision and quality enhancement based upon research. It also addresses the needs of those research staff who have the duty of teaching research methods to (hopefully) a new generation of researchers.

Those who read the volume will obtain a working map of the landscape of research and be able to locate research within education, training and the wider area of social science research.

The aims of the book, therefore, are as follows:

1. to introduce the important methodologies and data collecting techniques
2. to provide a framework for the critical assessment of the quality and role of existing research as found in the research literature
3. to support involvement in research.

The above intentions are cached out in more detail in the various chapters of the book.

There are two parts to Chapter 1. The first deals with how researchers can best arrange their lives to conduct research. Consequently, the issue of scheduling tasks and time management in general are discussed. This emphasizes the importance of producing a calendar of jobs to be done so as to enable those engaged in research to retain some time for a working life and a social life. The second part of the chapter deals with the more specific problem of planning the piece of research. Planning involves the formulation of research questions as well as purposes. It may be that the research is being performed for a specific purpose, such as a higher degree or for publication in a scholarly journal. Usually the research proposal will need to be submitted for approval to some agency such as a school, faculty or research board. All these issues are discussed in this chapter.

Chapter 2 deals with the issue of how to obtain funds and gain access to conduct research, for it is often possible to seek and obtain financial assistance to help with the research. Sometimes this may cover the full cost of the research, but more usually it will cover expenses likely to be incurred such as travelling, stationery and computer time. Knowing the organizations involved in the sponsorship of research is essential to this search for funding. In addition, many institutions have staff development policies that provide time, courses, secretarial help, etc for those engaged in research activities. The ethical aspects of research in the social sciences are also considered in more detail in this chapter.

Increasingly, the conducting of research projects is becoming part of everyone's culture. Many overseas students engaged in higher degree studies at western universities can be confronted, often for the first time, with having to engage in research. Often these students have particular difficulties, such as contacting their tutors at regular intervals, or with 'English for academic purposes', and so on. A brief mention is also made of these issues in this chapter.

Chapter 3 deals with the wide variety of methodologies that have evolved to help with most types of research problem. It also looks at how the researcher can adapt a methodology to suit a particular issue at hand. Methods covered include surveys, ethnographic methods, case studies, action research, life history methods, historical research, etc.

The development of the various data collecting devices and techniques and how they can then be used is the subject of Chapter 4. These include observation notes and schedules, questionnaires, interviews, documents, tests, attitude scales, field notes, diaries, etc.

The analysis of both qualitative and quantitative data is discussed in Chapter 5. Reference is therefore made to basic descriptive and inferential statistics, although in no way does the chapter attempt to convert the reader into a statistician!

Chapter 6 deals with the research and subject literature and demonstrates how it can be used to provide practical help with the research and the necessary theoretical foundations to support the work. Reference to the role of abstracts and CD-ROM searches, as well as to the more traditional sources, are also described. In addition the chapter suggests to the researcher suitable strategies for managing their collections of literature and how these sources should be critically evaluated.

It has become comparatively common in recent years for researchers to undertake a study of a particular organization, often the one for which they work. It is the aim of Chapter 7 to identify and consider the different perspectives that can be used to analyse organizations, such as cultural and political approaches.

The links between quality improvements, monitoring, evaluation and action research are dealt with in Chapter 8. The routine use of research activities and findings for management and quality improvement of practice are a particular focus of this chapter.

The importance of reflecting upon one's research and upon one's performance as a researcher cannot be overstressed. This topic is considered in Chapter 9, a basic tenet being that the research process can always be improved upon.

As well as dealing with some of the more 'routine' uses of the computer, such as for word processing, spreadsheets, databases and desktop publishing, Chapter 10 considers the various software available for data analysis. Programs covered include SPSS, SAS, MINITAB, MLn, LISREL, NUD.IST and Ethnograph.

Virtually all research studies will end in a report of some kind, whether it be a dissertation, thesis, article or a report for a funding body. This part of the process is discussed in Chapter 11. The chapter deals with how such reports should be structured. The form of English necessary and the incorporation of tables, graphs and other forms of numerical data is covered. As the citing of references often proves to be a difficult issue the Harvard system is considered, along with other, less common forms of citation methods.

There are a variety of avenues for getting research published. Chapter 11 examines all types of publication, from the more prestigious refereed journals to locally produced 'house' journals. The chapter also discusses the requirements that editors and editorial boards impose upon contributors.

After the research project has been completed and written up it is rare for there not to be other studies worthy of follow-up. In such cases what mechanisms are open to the researcher to maintain the momentum?

What, for instance, are the best strategies for obtaining funding for further research and for creating a 'research culture' in an organization? These issues are also dealt with in Chapter 11.

ACKNOWLEDGEMENTS

Finally, as a recognition of their assistance, we wish to acknowledge the forbearance of our wives. Many colleagues and students too have assisted unintentionally in the writing of this book. We wish to thank them also.

1

Planning a Research Project

There are a variety of reasons why people decide to carry out a piece of research. For many it is the need (or desire) to obtain a higher degree as most universities require some sort of research project, even with so called 'taught' masters and doctorates. In other cases individuals, teams or organizations may need to know how effective their activities are and what can be done to improve them. In such instances the research carried out will probably be 'applied' research.

The wide variety of situations and issues requires researchers to be familiar with a fairly wide range of methodologies. Research may be a piece of in-depth work within one organization or it may survey a range of institutions in a more comparative way. The research may be a qualitative piece of work or it may make much use of quantitative data and statistical methods. There is no set 'standard' format for a piece of research. It really depends upon the purpose for which it was devised.

Given these concerns, one of the essential abilities of any researcher is that of making focused decisions about the research. There is no one route to a particular conclusion, it is up to a researcher to decide where they wish to go and how they are going to get there.

PLANNING THE PHASES OF A PROJECT

Probably one of the first tasks the researcher will have to face when starting a project is the management of their time. Conducting research takes time (a minimum of 12–15 hours per week), so what is going to be given up in order to find time for the research?

ACTIVITY

Write down a list of social activities that you were involved in last week and then place them in order of importance.

Against each activity, write down how much time you spent on it, and consider where you can find time to carry out the research. Which activities in your list will need to be curtailed in order to provide this time?

It is also very important to routinize the research by allocating a set time and place in order to carry out the work. This at least enables researchers to feel healthily guilty if they choose not to work on the project at a particular time!

Most of those involved in research say that units of at least a whole day are preferable to allocating, say, a period of three hours to the research. Even better is if one can allocate longer periods at a time. This will give 'real' time for working and writing and the reflection so essential to the research process. Of course, this is not always easy. Often one has to settle for much shorter periods of time, but this is definitely second best.

The way in which time needs to be allocated is largely determined by the type of research that is being conducted. Work that is heavily dependent on libraries and archives tends to make different time demands from field work.

One of the most important jobs in planning a piece of research is to list and schedule all the tasks that are going to have to be undertaken.

ACTIVITY

Imagine that you have the task of conducting a traffic census outside your place of work and then preparing a report. Indicate the tasks involved in carrying out this assignment.

Once a complete list of tasks has been developed the next job is to place an approximate period of time against each task and schedule the list into a logical, sequential order. The technique of doing this is called *Critical Path* (or *PERT* – programme evaluation and review technique) *Analysis* and is described in Howard and Sharpe (1983).

ACTIVITY

Take the tasks listed above for carrying out the traffic census and:

1. put an approximate time against each one to indicate how long it will take
2. put the tasks in a logical order, indicating which tasks need to be carried out first.

You now start to obtain a picture of your project.

Finally, the above schedule must be converted into a calendar. Some will start with the final date by which they have to have their report or thesis prepared, others start with the here and now and then work forward. Whichever way is chosen, this calendar will become the master plan for conducting the research. It is obviously not inviolate – modifications may need to be made from time to time – but at the very least it will provide a yardstick against which to measure the progress of the project. Be fairly generous with time-scales, however, for various problems and slippage are likely to occur. Don't be too ambitious.

Figure 1.1 is an example of part of a typical critical path diagram, which illustrates how scheduling can be done. The figure represents the early part of a research project in which a questionnaire will be developed and then used.

Having allocated time and produced a schedule for the research, the next task is to develop a more detailed plan, describing the actual research methodology in a little more detail.

THE ROLE OF THE RESEARCH QUESTION

A suitable starting point can be a research question. A research question is a way of explaining as sharply and as pithily as possible to yourself exactly what you are going to research and what you wish to find out. Sometimes this may simply be in the form of a null hypothesis.

A null hypothesis is an assumption of a neutral (non-causal or inter-active) relationship between two items. For example, one might wish to examine if there is any difference between rural and urban children in their interest towards biology. The null hypothesis might therefore be:

There is no difference between urban and rural children in terms of their interest in biology.

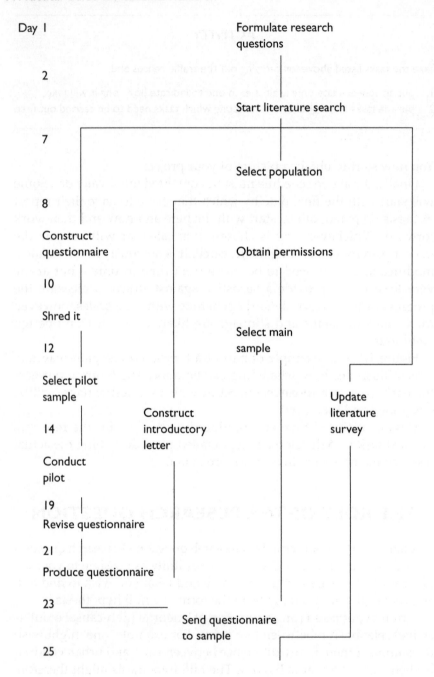

Figure 1.1 *A typical critical path*

The researchers would then have to develop a suitable 'scale of interest', sample equivalent groups of urban and rural children and see if there is any difference.

A null hypothesis of the type described above is often not suitable in the social sciences because one rarely has exactly comparable groups of the type suggested. Sometimes the research statement can be framed as a more general 'working hypothesis', but one will probably find few applications for such a strategy. More usually social science researchers are in a much more complex situation, where a research question will prove more suitable.

In general research questions should be *positive statements* which are *capable of being proven or not proven*. A statement which is a value judgement will not do, ie:

Geography is a more important subject than maths.

Similarly, a statement for which empirical evidence could not be obtained would not be suitable. An example of this might be:

Mathematics students in the twentieth century would score much higher in computer science examinations than would mathematics students of the nineteenth century.

A research question which presupposes the result would also not be appropriate, an example is:

I wish to show that my new reading curriculum is much better than the old one we used to use.

Research questions must therefore be framed in a positive manner, be value-neutral and be capable of being proven right or wrong on the basis of empirical evidence.

SOURCES OF RESEARCH QUESTIONS

Research questions are likely to come from three sources.

1. *Published books and articles.* Very often such publications will contain ideas for further research which can be framed into research questions. Alternatively, existing research will often throw up research questions other than those it answers.

2. Similarly, all *professionals and managers* will develop or have a wealth of experience. Reflections on this experience can often give rise to questions that can be answered by carrying out a piece of research.
3. Finally, *common-sense* issues arising from one's own expertise may be a good place to start.

FORMULATION OF RESEARCH QUESTIONS

The most important part of formulating a research question is to frame it at the correct level of abstraction.

A research question on organizational communication at differing levels of abstraction is illustrated below:

1. Is it possible to improve communication flow within this organiza-tion (in which I work)?
2. What specific factors enhance the understanding of current management policy and initiatives within this institution?
3. What specific factors enhance understanding of current management policy and initiatives by middle management in this organization?
4. What specific factors enhance understanding of current management policy and initiatives related to 'quality' by middle management in this institution?
5. What specific factors enhance understanding of current management policy and initiatives related to ISO 9000 by middle management in this institution?
6. What specific factors enhance understanding of current manage-ment policy and initiatives related to the development of work instructions related to the operation of switchgear under ISO 9000 by middle management in this institution?

The framing of the questions at level (1) or (2) are not really suitable as research questions. They are far too vague and do not give sufficient help on choice of methodology or what data collection techniques are likely to be needed. On the other hand, if a research question is produced that is too detailed, then it might be so specific that there is no real research project of substance possible. A research question set at about level (3) or (4), depending on how defined the question needed to be (and how much time and money is available), would be about right.

ACTIVITY

List three aspects of your own professional situation which might provide an interesting topic for a small piece of research.

Take one of the above topics and convert it into a research question at a suitable level of abstraction to enable you to formulate a research methodology.

Then indicate:

1. what is likely to be the most suitable methodology
2. what data will need to be collected.

It is important that the research question is stated as explicitly as possible. The research question should be sufficiently specific to enable *both* the methodology and the data collecting techniques relevant to the methodology to be formulated. If this is not possible then, in all probability, the research question(s) have not been specific enough in defining the exact question(s) they are trying to answer. It is worthwhile thinking through the research question in a little more depth before proceeding any further – this will save a great deal of trouble in the long run.

ACTIVITY

Below are some examples of research questions that could be improved. Read each one and then either improve it or delete it.

1. I wish to improve the training methods that are used in my electronics classes.
2. I need to compare the effectiveness of training programmes in AC circuit analysis for students in their first year of the electrical engineering course with a view to examining how well they provide practical skills for students in this subject area.
3. I need to show that group-based working is superior to whole class teaching for ten year olds studying mathematics.
4. I want to investigate the relative importance of learning science compared with learning art.
5. I wish to compare the response of pupils of 15 years of age to the comparative values of science and art as vocational subjects.
6. I need to compare the ability of engineering students in 1930 with those of today.

If the research questions above are problematic for different reasons, it is still essential to ensure a degree of specificity that is neither too great as to be unachievable nor too specific as to close down potentially fruitful avenues of investigation.

ACTIVITY

Examine the research questions below, which are at various degrees of specificity, and then decide which would be the most useful from the point of view of a potential researcher.

1. It is possible to improve the communication process in education and training.
2. What specific factors enhance understanding of current government policies and initiatives with respect to training?
3. What specific factors enhance understanding of current government policies and initiatives with respect to training within colleges?
4. What factors enhance understanding by lecturers of current government policies in relation to training in science and technology in technical institutions?
5. What factors enhance understanding of current government policies in relation to the teaching of digital electronics in technical institutions?
6. What factors enhance understanding of current government policies in relation to the teaching of digital electronics as applied to radar systems in technical institutions?

The focus in the research questions above is really about communication within organizations and, particularly, in educational and training institutions. In the examples, appropriate research questions might be those in the middle of the range (3, 4, 5); (1) and (2) are too general and (6) overly specific, unless (6) is defined as a closely focused case study.

ISSUES ARISING FROM THE USE OF RESEARCH QUESTIONS

This section addresses the question of what needs to be done after the research question has been constructed.

ACTIVITY

Having formulated a set of research questions, the following now need to be answered:

■ What is going to be the most suitable methodology to tackle this particular issue, bearing in mind any resource limitations which may exist?
■ What are the important strengths of this methodology?
■ What opportunities in terms of the research are offered by this methodology?
■ What threats or difficulties might this methodology impose?
■ What constraints does the methodology impose?
■ Having decided what is the most appropriate methodology, what data will I need to collect?
■ From whom shall I need to collect this data?
■ What data collecting instruments will I therefore need to develop?
■ What are the important questions which need to be asked?
■ What are likely to be the most promising methods of data analysis?

A useful reference here is Anderson (1990), which provides more details on this topic.

A related task might be to find someone of like mind with whom to collaborate, because working on one's own can be very lonely. A collaborator can considerably ease the burdens of the researcher and improve motivation and insight at critical times.

PERIODIC REVIEW AND REFLECTION USING RESEARCH QUESTIONS

As the research project proceeds, it is always a useful exercise to return periodically to the research question. Asking oneself 'Why am I doing this and what am I trying to find out?' can be a very salutary experience. Essentially then, the research question should explain to the researcher what they are going to do and how they are going to do it.

The formulation of the research question and the resulting plan of work are not necessarily going to be cast in 'tablets of stone'. The research process is almost always bound to require some ongoing readjustment. Research, after all, tends to be based on a series of decision-making points, though research questions establish a good baseline for decision making right from the outset.

ETHICS AND RESEARCH

Any research involving human (or, indeed, animal) subjects is bound to have important *ethical* implications. This is dealt with fully in a number of books (eg Burgess, 1989), and many research associations throughout the world have produced recommendations and guidelines on the ethical aspects of research methods in the social sciences. See Chapter 2, pp 24–25 for further details.

ACTIVITY

Identify at least four ethical issues that are likely to arise in the course of your intended research project and then list them.

Describe how you would attempt to deal with these.

GAINING ACCESS TO RESEARCH SITES AND DATA

It is important at the planning stage to ensure that all the data that it is intended to collect is, indeed, collectable. In some cases this will simply require that crucial stages in the research occur at times when the intended respondents are likely to be available (eg schoolchildren are not available during school holidays). Sometimes access may be required to an institution, or permission required to approach certain individuals or make use of published tests.

You must ensure that you establish who is responsible for granting such access or permission. It should be obtained, preferably in writing, before you start or early in the research process. Similarly, where a research programme requires the use of public or private archives or libraries, it is essential to ensure that they are open to researchers. Key factors may be times of opening and any fees for the use of the library or archive. It is not unusual for a small fee to have to be paid in order to become a member of a library. If you are intending to search a library or an archive it is useful to discuss requirements with a curator or librarian so as to ensure access to the most appropriate sources. It is very easy to miss valuable sources of information through ignorance of what is available.

Often, university research committees require letters permitting collection of the data before they will give permission for the intending research student or member of staff to commence the research. This is particularly true if the work is to be carried out for a higher degree.

For registration of higher degrees by research, the researcher is often required to produce and defend a plan (including the rationale) for the proposed research. In such cases it is necessary to explain as clearly and concisely as one can *what* you are going to do, *how* you are going to do it, *with whom* (ie the sample) you are going to do it and *why* (reference to seminal literature is appropriate at this point).

DEVELOPING INITIAL DATA ANALYSIS PLANS

An important aspect of the planning process to be decided early on in the research programme is how the data is going to be analysed. While this aspect is covered in more detail in later chapters, some preliminary decisions need to be made at the beginning of the research process. If the intended data is likely to be quantitative, it is very important to ensure that:

1. there are statistical methods available for dealing with the data
2. (and this can be almost as important) these methods are available on a standard computer package that is easily accessible to the person undertaking the data analysis.

If the intended data to be collected is qualitative, some initial decision about data format (how it is to be presented) is necessary in order to decide how to start the analysis. This will usually become apparent after a pilot stage, when sufficient data should be available to start making some decisions about the analysis.

The analysis of qualitative data does not usually require the use of computer-based methods, although packages have now appeared. Because of the complexities of most qualitative data normally it is not possible to devise a foolproof computer-based method of analysing it. However packages such as NUD.IST, Ethnograph and Hypersoft are very useful.

Remember, finally, that most research, unless it is very generously funded by outside bodies, is likely to be conducted on a small scale. This is particularly true of MPhil, MEd, MA and PhD projects. It is important not to be too ambitious in scope, but to make sure that the research makes an 'original' contribution to knowledge.

A WORD OF CAUTION

Research should not take over one's whole life, although for many researchers it does indeed become a way of life. On the other hand it would be wrong to suggest that research does not involve a fair proportion of the individual's time and resources. It is essential to be prepared to make some sacrifices.

2

Obtaining Funding and Access to Conduct Research

An important issue which faces the researcher at the start of their research is obtaining necessary resources to conduct the research. Resources usually come down to two principal factors:

1. How much *time* will be required?
2. What *funds* will be required to carry out the research?

There will, of course, be other considerations, such as the need to have access to working space, libraries and computer facilities, but usually these boil down to the two considerations of time and money. Indeed, having the time is often a case of having sufficient money to 'buy in' replacement staff to do the researcher's job.

It is therefore crucial to decide from the outset what resources are required and if these are likely to be available. If the researcher works within an institution of higher education research will probably be considered an integral part of their job specification; as a result they can expect to receive resources from their own institution. So one's own organization should be the first port of call. This is particularly the case if the research is either sponsored by the organization or will provide direct benefits to it (see Chapter 8).

It often happens that an organization – particularly a college or university – receives far more applications for funding than it has resources to fund. In such cases an application, though well constructed, may fail to receive funding. It is important at this point to realize that failure to attract funding from one's own institution does not necessarily mean that the project is not worthwhile. It is all a matter of priorities. Applicants should take due regard of all comments that may be made about the structure of a project proposal in such circumstances before seeking alternative funds. The essential thing is to continue to try if the first application is unsuccessful. This means learning from any mistakes made and modifying the proposal as necessary.

What sources of funding exist?

SOURCES OF FUNDING

There are quite a number of sources of funds, so one needs to devise a strategy in terms of making applications.

First, a decision needs to be made about whether or not to seek whole or part funding of the research. It might be better to ask for a smaller amount of funding for travel costs and/or secretarial costs, etc. In many cases whole funding is not available, as the individual researcher and/or their organization are expected to demonstrate some commitment by assisting with funds. Should one be successful with part funding decisions still have to be made on how to fund those parts of the project which are not in receipt of money. If the salary of the researcher remains their own responsibility or that of the employing institution it is crucial to ensure that one's line manager is aware of the application and of its implications. It would be most unfortunate to be in receipt of a grant but find that insufficient time was provided by the institution to complete the research.

The second decision to be made is to decide whether one should approach one of the larger 'general' funding agencies within countries such as (within the UK) the Economic and Social Research Council, Leverhulme or Nuffield, or one of the more specialist foundations. These latter may specialize in particular geographical areas (eg Anglo-German collaboration) or particular research foci (eg private companies or public agencies such as local authorities, Training and Enterprise Councils, trade unions and charities). In the USA the decision comes down to whether one should seek funding from federal, state or other non-federal sources such as foundations, some of which are private and some are public. Finally, do bear in mind that various regional organizations (eg the European Union) have projects and sources of income available for suitable projects.

In all cases it is important to be aware of the criteria that such foundations may impose with regard to type of research, size of grant, research area and, indeed, geographical area. Ries and Leukefeld (1995) provide more details of sources of funding in the USA and how to make bids for funds.

The larger general funding agencies tend to be much more well known to researchers and consequently are inundated with applications. It is difficult for the new researcher to secure research funding from such bodies unless the proposal really does break new ground.

Allied to the above considerations are whether one should approach a large or small organization for funding. The researcher must do some initial fact finding to establish the grant-providing record of the particular organization with respect to monies donated and areas of research and methodologies supported. As applying for grants is a time-consuming process it is essential that time is not wasted by making applications which are unlikely to succeed. Many countries have directories of grant donors that provide comprehensive lists of grant-awarding organizations.

The final consideration, having established which are likely to be the most promising grant-awarding bodies in the area, is whether one should attempt to secure all the funding required from just one body (with perhaps only a small chance of success) or separate out the various parts of the bid – eg travel, secretarial help, library access – and then make a separate bid for each of these items from a different body. The guiding principle here is that one is more likely to be successful with a small bid for funds than with a much larger one. A problem which can arise, however, is the one of uneven success. One can envisage a situation where there is funding for secretarial assistance to process data but no funding for travel to collect the data. This can place the researcher in a difficult and embarrassing position. It is not recommended that the bid is subdivided to too great an extent.

TYPES OF FUNDING

There are three types of funding regime available from grant-awarding bodies.

1. *Commissioned research*. Here the commissioning organization, in fairly precise terms, provides projects which it will support. Typically the organization then invites bids by competitive tender for the research. Evaluation research is often commissioned in this way. Those tendering need to be fully familiar with the area and with the methodology envisaged. They must be able to organize and conduct the work and usually have a track record in the area and the methodology.
2. *Responsive research*. Some grant-awarding organizations indicate general areas of research activity in which they are prepared to provide funding and then invite researchers to present suitable projects which fall within these areas. Grant-awarding bodies,

however, are increasingly specifying the areas in which they want research to be conducted.

3. *Canvassed research.* This is probably the format favoured by most researchers. Essentially the idea for the research comes from the researcher(s), who seeks to secure funds from an agency for all or part of the research. If the idea is a good one and the planning is good a researcher may well be successful. Unfortunately, such funding opportunities are becoming increasingly rare.

CRITERIA FOR THE ALLOCATION OF FUNDS

Most applications for research funding are subject to competition. There is a limited amount of money available and so there will be losers. Proposals are usually subjected to peer review to decide their merits. Research plans and costings are submitted anonymously to other researchers in the area who will comment upon, criticize and prioritize the proposals. These comments will often be passed back to the applicants to help them with further bids, although this is by no means a universal practice as funding bodies themselves do not have a great deal of money to provide this service. As with applications for internal funding, failure to secure a grant does not necessarily mean that the application was a poor one.

What aspects of the plan are the referees required to scrutinize? Normally all aspects are open for discussion, and each funding body usually produces its own set of guidelines for referees. Areas of importance on which referees are asked to comment tend to be:

- originality of the proposal and the contribution it will make towards advancement of theory in the area
- contribution made to improvements in methodology
- practical importance and significance of the proposal
- costings and time-scales
- how the research will be disseminated.

MAKING A BID FOR FUNDING

There are four substantial components to constructing a good bid for funding.

The first is that applicants must show that they have a track record in the particular area and/or in the particular methodology in which they are seeking funding. This statement might seem somewhat contradictory, since how does one obtain such a track record unless research funding can be secured to obtain it?

Other track record criteria include:

- the achievement of external funding in other, perhaps related areas
- good record of publications
- presentations at conferences.

Consequently it is very important to include past successes in any grant application. In fact all researchers should maintain a file in which they keep records of their success in their professional life, since invariably funding bodies will require CVs of all those named in a grant application. It is therefore also essential to have the expertise within the team to cover all aspects of the current application.

The second component should be a clear plan of work indicating such items as methodology, sample sizes, type of data collecting instruments to be used, existing facilities that are necessary and available to the researchers and any other funding sources. This plan should include a realistic timetable of activities. It is important that the plan does not try to cover too ambitious an area or time-scale with respect to the funds being sought.

Third, there should be precise and exact costings. Funding bodies normally require applicants to cost all aspects of the project in terms of facilities required, travel, secretarial assistance, materials, etc. The time of the researchers should be included in the bid unless the employing institution is definitely prepared to waive this cost.

Finally, since the bidding process is usually competitive, it is important to indicate what is unique and original about the proposal. Does it provide information which is of great and significant social importance? Does it make a fundamental contribution to practice or to methodology? Is theory moved onwards by the project? These are issues which need to be stressed in the project bid.

CONSTRUCTION OF A BUDGET FOR FUNDS

The budget breakdown should be as accurate as possible, and the items which should be included are as follows.

- *Staff time.* This should include costings for all staff involved in the project on the basis of what it would cost to buy in replacement staff. Staff development costs should also be included, and these can be considerable in a research project.

- *Secretarial assistance* and any *research assistants* employed, eg to conduct interviews. The employment of more than one research assistant would only normally be considered for a major project. Often secretarial assistance may not be great if the researcher is contemplating typing up their reports, data, etc on their own word processor.
- *Equipment*. With a research project in the social sciences this item often amounts simply to a computer and the associated software. However, it might include items such as tape recorders, video-recorders and radio microphones for fieldwork.
- *Working space*. Some organizations require their research staff to budget for office space on the basis of a cost per sq m. In addition, the researcher may well require a quiet room in which to conduct interviews, hold focus group meetings, etc.
- *Office sundries*. It is difficult to give a comprehensive list here, since it could be so varied, but items such as the purchase of stationery and hire of a photocopier would be included.
- *Travel and subsistence* including attendance at any conferences should be included.
- *Data input and analysis*. These could be quite expensive items if a large-scale survey is being considered. The researcher should consider carefully the use of such devices as bar codes and optical reader mechanisms to automate this process where the scale of the project warrants it.
- *Access and subscriptions to libraries and information centres*. Many archives allow free access, but charges are increasingly being levied. Often this charge is in the form of payment for membership. A decision therefore needs to be made about who and how many will require membership.
- *Cost of report preparation*. Some of the costs here may well be subsumed under some of the headings above, but typing time, stationery, binding and presentation, and assessment by externals may all be involved in this process. This will necessitate a consideration of what form the final outcome will take, which could be one (or more) of:
  - an article for a professional or refereed journal
  - a presentation at a conference
  - a report or a book
  - a seminar and/or course in which the results of the work are publicized to a wider audience.

In presenting these costings one obviously needs to demonstrate value for money. In particular, in large institutions, it is crucial that use is made of available facilities. An audit should be conducted of existing skills and facilities within the institution.

It is also necessary in this process to distinguish fixed costs. The cost of a computer might be spread across a number of projects; consequently only a part of its costs need be apportioned to the particular research project for which application is being made. Variable costs apply to salaries of researchers, stationery, etc. The cost in this case is in direct proportion to the amount used. Allowance should be made for depreciation of items such as computers and computer software, as the value at the end of the research period could be considerably less than it was at the beginning. The difference between the initial cost and the final value would then need to be borne by the research project if the piece of equipment was used wholly for the project during the period.

ASSESSMENT OF PROJECT BIDS

In constructing the research proposal it is very useful to have some idea of the criteria that will be used by the assessing panel to rate the proposal. These vary between different funding agencies, but some of the common criteria are given below.

- Does it fit the agreed policy of the school/department/faculty/ funding agency?
- Is it a good, rigorous research plan using appropriate method-ologies and data collecting instruments? Is the time-scale sensible?
- Is it correctly and realistically costed?
- What is the potential for attracting further funding?
- What is the quality of the bid and, in particular, how does it advance:
  - theory
  - methodology
  - knowledge
  - practice?
- How will the results be disseminated?
- Do the applicants have a good track record in this area with respect to research publications and attracting funding and are they there-fore likely to deliver the project in the agreed time-scale?

ACTIVITY

Prepare an application for a grant to a funding body for a piece of small-scale research lasting for two years and requiring your own time along with that of two part-time assistants.

Think carefully about any equipment and stationery that will be required.

Also consider what experience and qualifications you will require of the assistants so that an acceptable level of pay can be offered and, hence, a realistic costing can be made.

Ries and Leukefeld (1995) provide a great deal of more detailed help with the whole process of making applications to grant-awarding bodies, including the refereeing part of the process.

ETHICAL ISSUES

Most of the professional organizations in the social sciences (eg AERA, BERA, American Psychological Association, British Psychological Society, British Sociological Association, American Sociological Association) have drawn up ethical guidelines. Researchers should refer to these bodies for up-to-date copies of their guidelines and account should be taken of these when constructing the bid and when carrying out the research project.

Broadly, research ethics cover the following issues.

Respect for persons involved

Within the social sciences this relates to the respondents, who will usually be human although animals may be involved in a small number of studies. In either case there are guidelines relating to the physical and psychological well-being of the subjects. In particular, a person's confidentiality must be respected. It should not be possible to identify a respondent (or, indeed, an institution) from the completed report. It is the right of every respondent not to take part in the research if they so desire. Respondents who have provided information should have the opportunity of checking that it is an accurate statement of what they have said or written. This is not only desirable ethically but is a useful check on the veracity of the data.

Respect for truth

This particularly important with respect to data collection and analysis. In both processes authenticity is required – bias should not be introduced.

Openness

Readers of the final report should be given as much information as possible about how the data was collected (sample size, sample source, data collecting and analysis methods). However, it is still important that the point above relating to confidentiality is maintained and, if the two are in conflict, the confidentiality criterion should have higher priority.

Record keeping

It is essential that records should be kept of data collected (when, where, how and from whom) to aid validity and reliability checks. Records of expenditure (including receipts received) should be maintained for auditing purposes.

ACTIVITY

1. List at least four ethical issues which are likely to arise in your preferred research project.
2. Write down briefly your strategy for dealing with them.

SUPERVISING AND CONDUCTING RESEARCH OVERSEAS

The researcher may well find him or herself working in a different part of the world from where they are normally based. This could involve either conducting one's own research or supervising a research student overseas. This situation will obviously bring additional insights and opportunities but also, possibly, difficulties. The researcher therefore needs to plan carefully and build additional time into the project to allow for the unfamiliarity with local conditions and any additional problem-solving activities required.

The importance of good planning cannot be overstressed. The researcher needs to go through every step of the proposed research plan and ensure that resources and materials are available to complete each step on time and in the correct sequence. It is also very important to be aware of local customs. At the very basic level this will mean knowing the dates of public holidays, religious days, etc, and being aware of local customs (eg greeting respondents, use of language). It would be impossible to list all of these customs, but they are important. The most common do's and don'ts are contained in travel guides (Berlitz, Baedeker, Blue Guides, etc) available from bookshops. In addition, some attempt to master the basics of the local language is *always* useful.

It is also highly desirable to be aware of such issues as the local organization of education and training systems. In some countries, for instance, it is often the case that a head teacher may also be the owner of the school. This can obviously affect any research relating to school management. Similarly the general economic level of the population may be much lower than that in western countries and therefore questions relating to facilities available need to be framed with this in mind. This may also mean that questions normally asked in one country, such as choice of topics in the curriculum, may be completely irrelevant in a country which has a very centralized, hierarchical educational structure. It is therefore very important to obtain suitable briefing (for instance from the cultural attaché at the embassy of the country concerned).

In many countries conducting a piece of research, particularly for a higher degree, is unusual, so some explanation of why the research is being conducted might need to be given. This is particularly the case if one is undertaking research degree supervision or teaching, for instance on a taught Masters degree overseas, where the role of self-directed research is not always well understood.

Another issue is the maintenance of contact. The first essential is that mailing systems, telephones, faxes and e-mail or, at least, a sensible combination of these are going to be readily available. It is a good idea to carry out a preliminary audit of the facilities available for the research.

Similarly, it is important to ensure that communication systems within the country in which the research is being conducted are adequate, certainly for the efficient collection of data by questionnaires, etc. If possible, a group of at least two researchers should be convened within each country, to both help the research process and be mutually supportive.

Transmission and processing of quantitative data is made much easier between two countries and, indeed, between two institutions within a single country if uniform methods are used. Use well-known software packages such as Excel, SAS, SPSS and MINITAB and ensure that data sets are stored on disk to make them accessible to all. Where it is intended to produce the final report or thesis/dissertation in English it is imperative that all involved have a good facility in the four basic skills of speaking, reading, listening and writing.

ACTIVITY

Visit one or two libraries in the vicinity of your home or place of work and locate each of the following:

1. a reference book
2. at least four books in your subject area published within the past six years
3. six journals related directly to your area of interest, one of which should be an abstracting journal
4. at least one set of conference proceedings related to your subject area
5. one of the standard CD-ROM information sources
6. e-mail, fax or internet sources.

It is possible to devise one's own tests of these language skills, but there are tests and testing services available to make an individual assessment of a potential student's ability, particularly with the English language. The various testing regimes include International English Language Testing System (IELTS), Teaching of English as a Foreign Language (TOEFL), Oxford and Cambridge Examinations and Assessment Council and Northern Examinations and Assessment Board (NEAB).

Finally, researching overseas can have its challenges but the results, particularly in areas of comparative education, can be very beneficial to all involved.

3

Research Methodologies

One of the essential issues of any research project is knowing how to plan it. It is very important to have a perceived route through the territory. Obviously one cannot be completely clear about where the research will go, for often issues will arise that could not possibly have been foreseen at the beginning of the research process. In fact, it is the mark of a competent researcher to be able to respond to the data and to change direction should the need arise.

THEORY AND ORIGINALITY

One of the more complex issues with which a researcher has to grapple is that of originality. This is particularly the case if the person concerned is working for a research degree or making an application to a grant-awarding body. The subject of originality is often bound up with theory, since this is often one of the ways in which the originality of a programme can be stressed.

What is meant therefore by the term 'originality' when it is applied to a piece of research? There are a variety of definitions (eg Phillips and Pugh, 1994) and, indeed, a researcher can demonstrate originality in a number of ways.

1.   The research might make a contribution to theory in some way.
2.   The research might demonstrate methodological advance either in terms of a new methodology *per se*, an innovative use of an existing methodology or in the development of a new or novel data-collecting instrument.
3.   It might be an existing methodology applied to a group of respondents who had not previously been part of the sample.
4.   It could be original in terms of being a re-evaluation of existing research, possibly using different methods of data analysis.

5. It could be updating in some way an earlier piece of work.
    (This issue is discussed again in Chapter 11, which addresses the writing of the final report.)

The first point above perhaps requires a little more explanation. The traditional view of theory was the existence of a set of interrelated constructs or variables that gave shape to the particular research problem being studied. Often some type of model (physical, mathematical, etc) was involved. The relationship between the various component parts was also part of the theory.

To some extent theories only make sense within the particular paradigm in which they are presented. A traditional theory, for instance, based upon objective variables that exist 'out there' irrespective of the existence of the observer, would probably have little meaning within a research paradigm that was essentially constructivist (eg a phenomenological paradigm). If one were taking this more traditional view of theory the research programme might well be concerned with confirming or refuting the validity of the theory with the particular sample with which one was working. Alternatively the research might aim to modify existing theory by demonstrating that some variables were more important than others in determining causes, or that there were additional variables from those originally formulated which the theory failed to take into account.

A second view of theory and theorizing is that in which one seeks to establish theory anew, so to speak, from the data that has been collected in the research. This type of theory construction is often referred to as grounded theory (Strauss and Corbin, 1989) and is very popular in the social sciences.

ACTIVITY

Go to the library and find one example of a traditional theory and one example of a grounded theory in a social science context.
    Indicate what are the strengths and weaknesses of each type of theorizing.

In order to develop a suitable theoretical base for the research, it is essential to have access to library sources. These are dealt with in Chapter 6, but there are a number of issues which must be confronted at a fairly early stage of the research. For instance, it may be necessary to consult a range of primary, secondary and statistical sources, so the researcher will need to know:

1. Where are the sources located?
2. Is access to the sources and/or archives available at convenient times?
3. Are these archives available to bona fide researchers?
4. What costs are likely to be incumbent upon the research?
   (Many libraries make a charge to the researcher for locating and then transporting sources; others require the reader to take out membership of the library.)
5. What photocopying facilities are available?

Researchers need to ensure that they do not contravene any copyright law which applies to most of the materials that a researcher would wish to consult. If the materials are of historic importance it is likely that photocopying may not be possible anyway, due to the frailty of the materials. In addition, many libraries that contain archives allow the use only of pencils to record sources. It is most important to comply with all library and/or archive regulations.

METHODOLOGY AND PARADIGMS

It is helpful to look at methodology as a decision-making process that is predicated upon sets of background assumptions or paradigms. A paradigm is a theoretical model within which the research is being conducted, and organizes the researcher's view of reality (though they may not be aware of it!). Reality may be perceived as something which is individually constructed (ethnomethodology), as an objective 'out there' phenomenon (positivism) or a mixture of both (realism).

Where reality is defined within the first paradigm the related research will probably involve a great deal of individual discussion with respondents to understand their view of reality (what the situation is). If it is the second, objectivist paradigm the researcher assumes that all respondents will view the same events in more or less the same way. So, what might be true for a randomly selected, unbiased sample will probably be true for the much wider population from which that sample is selected. In the realist paradigm there will be underlying shared situations and experiences, but different interpretations. Research will thus seek to draw out the underlying experiences but also divergencies in perceptions of those experiences. It can thus be seen that the paradigm within which one works will have an important effect upon the methodological approach chosen (see Schwandt, 1997).

A second related term is methodology. This will to some extent be dependent on the type of paradigm within which the work is conducted. Positivist paradigm researchers tend to make more use of quantitative, experimental methods, while ethnomethodological paradigm researchers will make much more use of qualitative methodologies.

QUALITATIVE AND QUANTITATIVE METHODOLOGIES

Methodologies can be classified in various ways. Some writers (eg Cohen and Manion, 1994) distinguish between qualitative and quantitative methodologies reflecting the distinction between the various paradigms discussed earlier. Others differentiate between interventionist and non-interventionist research strategies (eg Carr and Kemmis, 1986). In the former the researcher actually 'does something' to or in the situation that is being studied. Both experimental and action research methodologies would be included here. In fact many of those methodologies described as 'scientific' or 'positivist' could be considered to be interventionist in some way.

A typology of some of the more common methods used in social science and education research is given below.

- Experimental
- Survey
- Developmental
- Action research
- Qualitative research:
  - Ethnography
  - Critical ethnography
  - Case studies
  - Evaluations
  - Historical research

- Policy research
- Market research
- Biographical studies
- Tracer studies

A brief summary of some of the more important methodologies listed above will now be given.

Experimental research attempts to control the situation so that (as far as is possible) only one item (or variable) of interest is isolated or studied. If (for instance) it was considered that computer simulations might be a better method of training electronics technicians than more traditional methods based upon lecture room, laboratory and workshop work, an experiment could be devised in which two equivalent groups could be formed. One group (the control group) might be taught by the traditional methods while the other group could be taught using the computer simulations. Both groups of students would be taught essentially the same curriculum. At the end of a specified period, say six months, the two groups could be compared using an appropriate assessment method.

The basic arrangement, therefore, when employing this methodology is to have a minimum of two equivalent groups that differ only in respect of the variable that is being investigated. Because the process of determining that the groups are equivalent may involve initial testing (although many researchers try to achieve this by random sampling) more refined methodologies have been constructed to control for any initial 'sensitization' this process may cause. Examples are the 'Solomon four group design', 'factorial designs', 'Latin' and 'Græco-Latin designs'. Many of these methodologies are described in Campbell and Stanley (1966) and Miller and Wilson (1983). Such methods are no longer used to any great extent in research in education and training, though they do have a place when suitable conditions for their deployment exist.

ACTIVITY

What practical difficulties are likely to arise from attempting to apply the experimental method of research to a typical teaching situation?

A number of difficulties will be immediately apparent if one tries to apply the experimental methodologies.

1. There is often the difficulty of forming and managing comparable groups in the first place, especially if the situation demands the involvement of other staff in addition to the researcher. This is likely to cause problems since the other staff will, in effect, constitute an additional variable which cannot be controlled.
2. The methodologies assume that any one variable (in this case the teaching method) can be isolated. All other variables are required to be controlled, yet it is very difficult, within the normal exigencies of many situations, to control every confounding variable. Variables such as ability, level of motivation and background are almost impossible to control in most situations.
3. Similarly it would be very difficult to isolate the two groups in order to prevent cross-referencing of their classroom experiences.
4. It is well known that any new method will often appear successful when it is first used simply because it is novel to the subjects. After periods of time new methods often cease to motivate the subjects and performance drops.
5. What is known as the 'Hawthorne' effect often also applies. This occurs when subjects change their performance simply because they know that they are the subject of an experiment.
6. An important deficiency of the above research study is that, while on completion the researcher may have 'proved' that one pedagogical method is superior to another, there may still be no indication of *why* that method is superior. The researcher may be no wiser in terms of pedagogic theory.
7. Finally, the method described above takes no account of the ability of respondents to *speak for themselves* and thus explain what is particularly valuable and effective for them about the various teaching methods. It would not be impossible to build this into the methodology by interviewing a number of the respondents, but to do this is to alter the methodology. If this *were* done much more insight would be gained into the teaching, thinking and motivational processes involved.

Correlational research is related to the experimental method. This method looks not at the difference between two (or more) groups but at the relationships between two (or more) variables. For instance, is there a relationship between a student's ability in mathematics and their performance in science? To answer this question one might set a given group of students tests in both areas and then see whether the two sets of results demonstrate a relationship (correlate). While there may be evidence of a relationship it is not necessarily a *causal* one since there might be intervening variables or an inverse correlation.

Survey methods are particularly useful to get an overview of a particular situation and are often used by policy makers and by those who wish to inform policy makers. A survey of schools might reveal that 70 per cent of primary schools are generally teaching reading in a good or satisfactory way. This would be valuable information for the policy maker. It would be less useful for the individual teacher or school unless they know (which they often do not) into which category their school is placed.

Developmental methods are usually interesting because they study an attribute or attributes of a particular cohort over a specified period of time. The main issue for the researcher is the sensibility of the proposed time-scale. It might be very interesting and valuable to study development in the ability to speak French over the course of four years, but this implies that the total time required for the research will be at least four years. With the setting up and writing up, the final report may well take in excess of six years. This is hardly likely to be a practical proposition for many researchers.

Cross-sectional studies are one way of avoiding this time problem. What this means is that, in a given year, the researcher would examine the French-speaking ability of four groups who had been learning to speak French for one, two, three and four years respectively. This makes the construction of the time-scale easier, but it does assume that this year's year two will be equivalent next year to this year's year three. This is difficult to ensure. One variant of the developmental study is *ex post facto* research (Cohen and Manion, 1994). Here, one looks at a current situation, eg the degree of success which a group of 18 year olds might have had with their university entrance examinations, and then research backwards in time to try to identify those variables in their life histories (study methods, etc) which might account for their success (or lack of it).

Action research is research conducted by a professional into their own activity with a view to bringing about an improvement in their practice. An instructor might diagnose an issue with one of their groups, analyse their own instruction and, on the basis of this, implement and evaluate a possible solution to the issue. Data would be collected to check how effective the strategies had been. This is a very valuable form of research and should lead to an improvement in practice. However, as the research problems are discrete and organizationally bounded it is difficult to generalize, because every class is different – what may work with one group may well not work with another.

It is possible to establish some general principles in action research which are transferable to other, similar situations. Essentially action research is a cyclic process where one is continually modifying aspects, collecting data for evaluating change and, on the basis of the results, implementing further strategies. Potentially action research never stops, although the researcher who is aiming for a higher degree or an article will have to make the painful decision to stop at some point, even if only temporarily, in order to write up the research.

Action research as a methodology dates back to the positivist research of Lewin in the 1940s (Adelman, 1993). By way of contrast Stenhouse (1975) moved the methodology towards a more qualitative, research-based approach. The apparent conflict between qualitative and quantitative methodology was sidelined to some extent in the following years by the perceived need to use action research as a means of identifying what is 'distinctive' about research in the area of education and training (Carr and Kemmis, 1986). It was Elliot (1991) who brought action research back into the classroom. Jean McNiff (1988) has given an account of the history of action research practice, noting the work of the philosopher Habermas to provide a socio-political dimension to the methodology. Action research methodology has become much more 'eclectic' in its approach, and both data collecting methods and theory construction (grounded theory, scientific theory, explanatory theory) have been much more flexibly interpreted.

Qualitative methodologies are very varied. *Ethnographic* methods embodied in case studies, evaluations and biographical studies are popular. For a researcher hoping to use any of these methods there are many specialist books with good examples of such research in action. Both Hammersley and Atkinson (1983) and Fetterman (1989) provide excellent explanations of the term 'ethnography' and the methods, techniques and methods of data analysis appropriate to this methodology. Other well-known researchers in this area are Paul Willis, Andrew Pollard, Peter Woods, Anselm Strauss, Jayne Spradley and Robert Burgess. Hitchcock and Hughes (1995) discuss ethnographic research techniques in education.

The methodological approach of ethnography can be difficult for researchers used to a more objective scientific method of research. The role and place of theory, in particular, can be hard to understand. Different ethnographers have different views on this with, some rejecting a place for theory altogether. Fetterman (1989) says:

> Typically, ethnographers do not make a grand theory explicit, because they do not automatically subscribe to one. A grand theory can be instructive, but many ethnographers find it unwieldy and unresponsive to day-to-day research needs. (p17)

Fetterman also distinguishes, as do many other ethnographers, between *emic* and *etic* perspectives. The former assumes that the actors each have their own reality of the situation so there is no single reality for all of them. The latter (etic) view tends to view reality in a more object-ivist, single view.

Critical ethnography, one form of ethnography, has become popular recently. Most of the conventions of the ethnographic method are shared with critical ethnography, but the latter tends to involve a more active micro-political engagement in the situation being studied. The emphasis in critical ethnography is upon linking structures and percep-tions, upon emancipation rather than upon description and explanation. Thomas (1993) in particular described critical ethnography in more detail.

Case studies are both an approach to reporting research and also a methodology that concentrates upon singular or small numbers of individual instances. Case studies may be of an individual or individ-uals, institutions (or discrete, definable parts of an institution) or of situations or particular types of provision (eg a curriculum or training development).

Case studies, by their very nature, study singular phenomena. There are examples of 'multiple case studies' but these would not claim necessarily to be representative. Indeed, a case study may be a case study precisely because it has an exceptional (the exception) emphasis. The aim of any case study is to describe and understand the pheno-menon 'in depth' and 'in the round' (completeness). In this function case studies do serve a useful purpose, since many important issues can be overlooked in a more superficial study such as a survey.

The relationship of the data collected to theory in case studies can be problematic. Usually the researcher will not aim to develop 'scientific theory', since large samples will not have been selected. However, it is possible to develop grounded theory and to use the results to hold a mirror to existing theoretical perceptions and writings on, for instance, organizations and how they operate. The data collection and analysis methods are those normally encountered within other forms of qualitative research but the emphasis is on small-scale instances of phenomena. Both Yin (1994, 1993) and Stake (1995) have described the methodology in some detail.

Much applied research takes the form of either an *evaluation* or *market research*. Both are legitimate forms of research and use the range of methods of data collection and analysis. Hopkins (1989) provides a good review of both the theory and the practice of the former, while Green and Tull (1978) discuss the latter.

One can also link *policy research* and *historical research*. The data collecting methods in these approaches are based much more on accessing documentary sources, which are a prime requisite. Sources for such research are dealt with in the next chapter, but the books by Kitson Clark (1968), Kragh (1987), Scott (1990), Barzun and Graff (1992) and, for those interested in local issues, Campbell-Kease (1989) are useful starting points. The subject of policy research has been described in detail by Majchrzak (1984).

The treatment of historical subjects has changed somewhat over recent years, away from the more hagiographic views towards attempts to understand contemporary events for members of the public of that time. Moreover, a great deal of historical research is concerned now to explain events within the social context pertaining to the time. It is therefore invaluable to look at the treatment of historical issues in recent articles in journals such as *History of Education* and *British Journal of Educational Studies* to see how these are handled.

Biographical research is a more recent innovation. It tries to gain an understanding of respondents and their actions by examining their life (or part of their life) story. Offredy (1995) has conducted biographical research into trainees entering government-sponsored youth training schemes, whereas Warren (1987) has examined why so few women have tended to enter the profession of engineering. A plethora of data collecting techniques is possible, ranging from simply asking individuals to write down their life story to unstructured and more structured interviewing, discussions, diaries, participant observation and questionnaires (Offredy, 1995).

Some of the techniques involve the use of *critical incidents* or 'epiphanies', identifying crucial decision-making points in an individual's career path or personal life (Tripp, 1993). While respondents can often be described as 'typical' of a group or category of person it is also interesting to investigate respondents who are not typical (eg the male who decided to become a kindergarten or infant school teacher or the woman who heads a university engineering school). Whereas ethnography tends to deal with the present situation and its context, the emphasis in biographical work is to look backwards to identify, if possible, the causes that may help to explain the current situation. As Hitchcock and Hughes (1995) explain:

The life history approach offers a clear potential in terms of considering the ways in which culture is moulded, changed and created by individuals through time. (p185)

It is essential when conducting biographical research to see the respondent as a complete person and therefore to take account of the respondent's life and the context of that life in its totality. Hitchcock and Hughes (1995) offer a critique of this methodological method. The use of flow diagrams and critical paths (see Miles and Huberman, 1994) is quite a useful way of making sense of the results of such research.

Tracer studies are also a more recent arrival on the scene, and have some of the characteristics of biographical study and the developmental studies discussed earlier. In essence they follow the development of individuals in their career paths. Fletcher (1996) has described how this can be done in a developing country, and provides useful information on aid agencies in understanding how their funds are deployed.

CONCLUSION: METHODOLOGIES AND SOME LOGISTICAL ISSUES

While this chapter has sought to provide an overview of the main categories of research methodologies, it should never be forgotten that the choice of methodologies is dependent upon both the subject of the research and the related aspects of the research design. The following activity reiterates the relationships between all these factors through the creation of a systematic research design. The exercise is well worth completing, if only as a dry run for an actual research proposal.

ACTIVITY

Assume that you are going to spend about one year on a research project with about 10–12 hours a week to devote to it. Prepare a research plan that is both realistic and achievable. Remember that this plan is simply a first draft and will need to be rewritten at a later date as the research proceeds. Your plan should make reference to the following items:

- There should be a clear statement of the problem hypotheses or research questions.
- What type of methodology and data collection are likely to be required?
- How will the data be collected?
- How might the data be analysed?
- Try and select a problem in which you are personally interested or in which you have a professional interest. Some possible ideas are presented below.
  - Are resources (both human and material) being allocated in the most appropriate way in my institution?
  - How can liaison between an educational institution and local industry/commerce be improved?
  - What is the best way of establishing a parent-teacher association?
  - How can communication be improved within an institution?

All research, then, needs to be planned correctly. For most types of research the essential point is to *think small*. Research projects often expand as time goes on, but they rarely contract.

Nothing has been said so far about the actual data collection and analysis processes. Often these are determined by the methodology chosen, for experimental methods often make use of achievement tests and psychometric tests; survey methods use questionnaires and interviews; historical methodology uses documents (primary, secondary and statistical sources) and oral evidence; while ethnographic and action research methods primarily use diaries, observations, discussions (focus groups) and interviews.

The next chapter discusses data collecting methods in much more detail, while data analysis is discussed in Chapter 5.

4

Data Collection

The data collecting part of a project is where many researchers feel the 'real' research occurs. Data collecting can be addictive, and can seriously endanger the health of the researcher and the completion of the research! Nonetheless the 'fieldwork' is where new information is acquired and its significance begins to be assessed.

Data collection is not just a process of collection, it is also a process of creation – of using information in unique ways related to the purposes of the study. There is a wide variety of data collecting methods available to researchers in the social sciences; deciding which to use will depend on:

- the particular methodology that has been selected (objectivist or constructivist, quantitative or qualitative (or mixtures of both))
- what is feasible in a given research situation
- what is likely to yield the most appropriate information.

All these items are decided upon in the context of the particular research problem.

Some of the more important data collecting methods are listed below.

- Questionnaires
- Observations
- Documents
- Accounts and protocols
- Tests
- Sociometry
- Action research
- Interviews
- Dialogue records
- Diaries and field notes
- Focus groups
- Repertory grid methods
- Attitude Scales
- Evaluation research
- Written and other works of various kinds (eg books, essays, computer assignments).

Many of these data collecting methods have alternative forms. Observations, for instance, may be participant or non-participant, while interviews may be structured, semi-structured or unstructured. Despite this variety there are some basic principles which apply to all data collecting methods.

BASIC PRINCIPLES OF DATA COLLECTION

First, any method must produce data that is relevant to the research question(s), and able to provide answers or illumination on the topic. Second, the technique must be convenient and relatively easy to use in the circumstances, for the researcher has to be sure that the expenditure of time (and resources) is warranted by the project. Perhaps most important, however, are issues of validity and reliability of the research techniques used.

Validity, reliability and ease of use

The person undertaking the research needs to be sure that the data collecting instrument is both *valid* and *reliable*. What is meant by these terms?

Validity

If the research technique is valid it is 'sound, cogent, well grounded, justifiable, or logically correct' (Schwandt, 1997). In simple terms, validity ensures that data sets collected or items used are pertinent or relevant to the research.

There are different types of validity. Miller and Wilson (1983) list the following forms of internal validity:

- face
- concurrent
- content
- predictive
- criterion related
- construct
- convergent
- discriminant.

ACTIVITY

Discover the meaning of each of the types of validity listed above and then decide how important each one is likely to be for the data it is intended to collect.
List the main *threats* to internal validity.

In the main, validity can be:

- internal or face validity (the techniques directly relate to the intended outcomes and concerns of the research)

or

- concurrent validity (the data collected is valid for the much wider population from which that sample is drawn)

or

- predictive validity (provides data that is useful for making predictions about the future behaviour of the research subjects in a causal or correlational manner).

In validity the concern should be to reduce the amount of interference by non-relevant or non-valid aspects, such as the language used. In research techniques such as interviews and questionnaires the language should not be overly complex and arcane, or hinder understanding and answering (responses).

Ensuring validity can be achieved in a number of ways, one of which is to carry out an initial investigation (a pilot study) using any intended data collecting instrument to check the authenticity and relevance of the data produced. Alternatively, a panel of experts can be used to assess that the planned instrument really does measure what it is supposed to be measuring. Alternatively again, there is the extent to which the results obtained with the research tool or instrument correlates with existing instruments said to measure the same or similar items. Where a valid test or instrument already exists, it is open to the researcher to use the existing instrument. Alternative instruments should only be developed if there are valid reasons for doing so. It is not necessary to reinvent the wheel all the time!

Some methods employ factor analysis to check validity. This approach is complex, and details can be found in Oppenheim (1992) and Kline (1994).

Finally, there is a convenient approach known collectively as *triangulation*. Essentially, with these, the researcher repeats the (pilot) study using alternative:

- data collecting instruments
- investigators
- methodologies
- units of analysis
- theoretical perspectives.

The central point of triangulation is to examine the research topic or focus from a number of different vantage points, though this should not blind the researcher to differences between sets of data that such different vantage points provide.

Reliability

Reliability is the second feature that any data collecting instrument must possess. Generally speaking it is usually much easier to measure reliability than validity. Miller and Wilson (1983) define reliability as:

> The extent to which a test would give consistent results if applied more than once to the same people under standard conditions. (p96)

One approach to check validity is the 'test-retest' method. This involves using an instrument (eg attitude scale, interview schedule) with a group on two separate occasions and analysing how closely the two sets of results conform to each other (provided the two occasions are not separated by an excessive time-scale). A significant correlation should be observed between the two sets of results. There might be some small differences between the two groups as respondents (the sample) are likely to change a little between the two occasions. One should not expect an exact replication of results.

The other method of assessing the reliability of an instrument is to split the results of a test or questionnaire into two halves and then measure how well the one correlates with the other. There are computer packages available that will carry out this procedure, for instance SPSS has Cronbach's Alpha, which works on the above principle.

Problems may still arise, however, for a test can be reliable but not valid. It is possible that a test may measure something other than what it is believed the test is measuring, in which case it is reliable but not valid because it would not be measuring what the researcher supposed it to be measuring.

Carmines and Zeller (1979), Kirk and Miller (1986) and Litwin (1995) all discuss the subjects of validity and reliability.

Ease of use

It is important that data collecting instruments are easy to administer. One can have an instrument that is valid and reliable but, if a single researcher (and usually it is just one) is unable to use it because of its complexity, the results yielded may still be suspect. Examples of such instruments are structured observation schedules, for instance in classrooms or workshops, which involve complex activities and interactions. Given this complexity and multiple simultaneous events, observation schedules that require a researcher to observe and classify what is going on at a particular time can be very difficult to operate. In such situations ease of use often has to be traded off against some loss of data.

Sampling populations and data collection techniques

Sampling populations

In the many cases where a researcher is unable to cover an entire population it becomes necessary to use a sample (subsection) of a population. Suppose one wished to examine teaching and learning methods in public training institutes throughout the UK. It would be impossible on a restricted budget and time-scale to examine all such institutes, and necessary, therefore, to focus on a small sample of such institutes representative of the whole population.

A sample can be:

■   random (every member within a population has an equal chance of being selected); random sampling may be simple (drawn from a hat) or systematic (eg every tenth individual in an alphabetical list)
■   stratified (clearly distinct groups within a population are represented)
■   cluster (geographical or other cluster (eg age/sex/occupation), assuming those sampled to be representative of the much larger population).

A related issue is that of sample size. Analysing data takes time, whether it is, for example, coding and collating questionnaire results or transcribing and coding interviews. If small effects are being investigated, or if the population is particularly heterogeneous and a high degree of confidence is sought, or if the sample is to be divided into sub-samples, then a larger sample may be called for. Whatever the case, the target should be a sample large enough to provide meaningful data but which is not excessively time consuming and invidious.

The issues of sampling are discussed in Kish (1965), Cochran (1977), Moser and Kalton (1971) and Cohen and Manion (1994).

Data collection techniques

Two of the most commonly used data collecting techniques are *questionnaires* and *interviews*. Some of the advantages and disadvantages that may help a researcher decide which method is more appropriate in a given instance are as follows.

Questionnaires	*Interviews*
Useful for simple topics	Useful for more complex topics
Possible to have large numbers of respondents	Time consuming
Anonymous	Not suitable for embarrassing issues
Often poor response rate	Usually good response rate
Emphasis on writing ability	Less emphasis on writing ability

Someone other than the researcher should scrutinize a questionnaire or interview schedule to eliminate unsuitable or ambiguous items. In addition, it is essential that the schedule or questionnaire is piloted on respondents who are as similar as possible to those in the group who will eventually be asked to participate. It is often helpful to go through a questionnaire verbally at the pilot stage, for this can provide information on irrelevant or poorly constructed items. At some point, however, it is also necessary to ask the pilot respondents to complete the instrument under conditions similar to the 'real' thing.

PLANNING QUESTIONNAIRES

Alreck and Settle (1985) and Oppenheim (1992), among others, provide a detailed account of how to tackle the construction and use of questionnaires and interviews. What follows therefore is a useful checklist.

- What are the essential questions (as distinct from those that one might like to ask)?
- What is the population frame (what groups or individuals comprise the respondents)?
- What sampling approach is to be used (random, systematic random, stratified)?
- What independent variables are going to be used in the analysis (eg sex/age/social class/job etc)?

- Is the questionnaire of an appropriate length (long questionnaires tend to have a smaller response rate)?
- Has the instrument been piloted?
- Is the instrument valid, reliable and easy to use?
- Has the instrument been piloted on a population as close as possible to that on which it is to be used?

Notwithstanding the need to avoid an overlong questionnaire, it is important to ask all the questions that need to be asked in one go. It is unsatisfactory to have to issue a revised questionnaire because all of the questions were not asked first time around or were badly formulated. This includes not only the direct, factual questions that need to be asked but also any information required to enable relationships to be analysed.

For the items in a questionnaire the following questions should be asked.

- Are there both negative and positive responses, and is there a reasonable balance between them?
- Are the items:
  - clear and free of ambiguities
  - free of over-complex questions
  - free of questions which contain more than one variable
  - free of leading questions
  - free of colloquial terms or slang
  - questions upon which the respondent has sufficient knowledge to answer
  - free of questions which ask for 'average' quantities (guesses)?
- Are the response modes used appropriate?
  A response mode might consist of:
  1. Nominal scales (eg *What type of car do you drive? Ford ❋ Chrysler ❋ Mitsubishi ❋*)
  2. Ordinal/Likert scales (eg *Mathematics is essential for all business studies students:*
     Strongly agree ❋ Agree ❋ Uncertain ❋ Disagree ❋ Strongly Disagree ❋)
  3. Interval scales (eg *What is your age?*
     21–26 ❋ 27–35 ❋ 36–45 ❋ 46–54 ❋ over 55 ❋)
  4. Ranked responses (eg *Rate the following aspects of your course in order of importance. Use '1' in the box for the most important, down to '4' for the least important).*
Teaching methods	▢
Content	▢
Meeting other training officers	▢
Refreshments	▢

5. Semantic differential responses (eg *Place a tick on the line below to show your opinion of refectory lunches:*
    BLAND _ _ _ _ _ _ _ SPICY)
6. Open responses (respondents are invited to write comments).

■   For the sample itself, how will respondents and initial non-responders be contacted?

(It cannot be assumed that those who initially fail to respond and have to be contacted a second time will produce the same answers to questions as those who responded at the first attempt. The former group of responses should be kept separately from the latter. Both groups of responses should then be examined to see whether there are substantial differences between the two.)

Coding and analysing questionnaires

While it may seem perverse to consider the coding and analysis of data at the planning stage of a questionnaire, this is worth doing, as it helps to clarify both the intent of questions and the most appropriate sort of response for analysis. Coding is the process of assigning a symbol as a shorthand way of summarizing a completed questionnaire response. Typically, numbers or letters are used in coding. An example of how results might be coded is given below:

Question: Which of the following training methods have you used in the past four weeks?

Group sessions
Computer-based training (CBT)
Case studies
Simulations
Lectures
One-to-one tutorials

		Group	CBT	Case study	Sims	Lecs	Tuts
Respondent	1	Y	Y	Y	N	Y	Y
	2	N	N	N	N	Y	Y
	3	Y	Y	Y	Y	Y	Y
	4	Y	Y	Y	Y	N	N
	5	Y	Y	Y	N	N	Y

OR

Respondent						
1	1	1	1	0	1	1
2	0	0	0	0	1	1
3	1	1	1	1	1	1
4	1	1	1	1	0	0
5	1	1	1	0	0	1

Numbers are often better to use than letters, as zero can be used for a non-response, and other numbers assigned to multiple response questions such as the semantic differential above.

Finally, it is important to consider how the data is to be analysed. Data analysis is discussed in Chapter 5, but as an advance organizer (the development of a framework or overview), the researcher should have some idea of what the independent and dependent variables are. In voting patterns, for instance, the age of the respondents might be the independent variable, and voting the dependent variable – people tend to vote for certain parties as they grow older.

ACTIVITY

The items below were taken from questionnaires; all of them could be improved. Read each item carefully and identify the main fault(s). How would you rewrite the item?

- Do you prefer to teach science to eleven year olds or mathematics to fourteen year olds?
- Do you prefer to read a quality newspaper such as the XXXX or a popular newspaper such as the YYYY?
- Do you have discipline problems in your classes?
- How often do you use computer simulation exercises in your science classes?
- How do you feel that your course of training prepared you for present teaching conditions and the current school curriculum?
- Does your child enjoy doing their English homework? (*A question for parents.*)
- To what extent has the reorganization of your local education authority/School Board been beneficial to work in the lower part of the secondary/high school?
- Do the pupils in your school prefer process type of teaching methods in science to the more didactic type?

In some types of questionnaire the issue of *attitude measurement* arises. There are basically three ways of constructing attitude scales: Thurstone scales, Guttmann scales and scales derived using factor analytical methods. These are dealt with fully in Oppenheim (1992), which should be studied before any attempt is made to measure attitudes.

PLANNING AND CONDUCTING INTERVIEWS

The intention here is to provide an overview. As with research topics, there are whole books (or large sections of books) devoted to interviews (eg Powney and Watts (1987), Oppenheim (1992) and Drever (1995)).

Planning interviews

What follows is a list of questions which indicate the main decisions and the order in which they should be taken.

- What are the research questions that are the focus of the interviews?
- Who are the sample?
- What interview method should be used (eg structured, semi-structured, unstructured)?
- What should be the format of the different questions and any necessary prompts/follow-up questions?
- How will responses be recorded (eg verbatim, note form, tape-recorded)?
- What are the possible methods of classifying the responses (eg open or axial coding)?
- Who and how many precisely should be interviewed (should they be typical or atypical or both)?
- How are respondents contacted?
- Where and how will the interviews be conducted (eg formal, informal, at home, etc)? (NB: If there is more than one interviewer briefing will need to take place at this point.)
- What protocols will be used in producing transcripts?

Once the interviews have been completed (or are ongoing), the researcher has to:

- produce transcripts
- code responses
- examine for patterns or otherwise analyse the results
- classify patterns and categories of responses

■ validate responses (ie check researchers' categorizations and conclusions against those developed by a colleague).

In using an interview schedule as a method of obtaining data an investigator needs to relate responses and analyses to any theories that exist or are being developed. It is also necessary to ensure that there is a representative group of respondents if this is likely to be a significant factor. Of course, in some cases, it is the aim to interview people who are not representative, eg the female head of an engineering department, the man who has trained to be an infant teacher. Here one may well be conducting biographical research to try to establish why they have acted as they have done.

Conducting interviews

As far as possible the interview should be relaxed but businesslike, with the respondents being put at ease, and the intentions of the interview clarified (though still trying to avoid interviewer bias, where the respondent gives the answers they believe are required rather than the truth). It is always very valuable to have prompts (additional questions) available for an interview. Prompt questions enable the interviewer to carry the interview forward should the respondent not be clear about the meaning of the question or be giving monosyllabic answers. Prompt questions should be included on the interview schedule before the actual interviewing begins so that the investigator can check that they do not lead the respondent in any way.

One interview technique often used with survey methodology is the Delphi technique. Here, respondents are asked a series of questions, their responses are collated and the researcher then returns to resurvey the respondents after they have received the results of the first survey.

A method often used with young children, particularly if the intention is to establish their understanding of specific concepts, is the 'Interview about Instances' method. Here the respondent is presented with instances and non-instances of concepts and asked to say if they agree that this is an example and to explain their reasoning. The technique is illustrated by Osborne and Freyberg (1985).

Focus groups are a popular way of collecting data. They are, in effect, group interviews, but use the interaction of group members to elaborate and expand upon the agreed focus of the meeting. Both Anderson (1990) and Krueger (1994) describe how to use this technique.

Focus groups need careful planning, as well as being composed of respondents who are both interested in and reasonably knowledgeable about the topic being researched. Open questions rather than closed ones typically are asked. The synergy of the group can then enable a much livelier discussion than would be possible in a one-to-one interview situation. In addition, once started, it is less likely that respondents will be 'led' by the interviewer. The composition of the group makes a difference. Krueger (1994) suggests that an optimum group size of 7–10 participants is the most effective.

OBSERVATION METHODS

Observation methods are very valuable in a wide range of research projects. They can:

- be structured or unstructured, focused or diffuse
- concentrate on dialogue or observed interactions or respondent characteristics, or combinations thereof
- be recorded using written notes, audio or visual (video) recordings.

The precise form of data collecting and recording will depend on the nature of the project and the resources available. There are, however, dangers in trying to record too much and in too great a detail. A structured observation schedule can be very useful because it focuses observations on activities directly relevant to the research question. For those new to the research process this can be of considerable help. By using structured schedules, however, the researcher extracts data from the situation and tends to impose their own interpretation on the situation, often preventing the actors from being able to 'speak for themselves'.

A number of publications give very detailed advice about how to use this means of data collection, eg Croll (1986), Jorgensen (1989), Edwards and Westgate (1994), Munn and Drever (1995), Foster (1996) and Sanger (1996). As well as observing workplace situations the observation method is also useful in management and other types of meetings, such as in the statementing procedures for certain special needs pupils.

ACTIVITY

Obtain an observation schedule (such as Flanders') and use it with an actual video-recording of a group.

Write down any difficulties that you experience in using the schedule.

How might the schedule need to be modified in order to overcome the difficulties discovered?

Degrees of structure are possible in using observation. Many ethnographers, for instance, aim for less rather than more structure. Hammersley and Atkinson (1983) suggest a range of degrees of involvement, from:

- 'complete observer'
- 'comparative detachment'
- 'objectivity and sympathy'
- 'comparative involvement'
- 'subjectivity and sympathy'

to

- 'complete participant'.

Involvement with a group can enable the researcher to uncover meanings and motivating factors that the more objective (external) observer might well miss, though there also may be a researcher effect on the group and the situation.

The reliability and validity of data is just as important in observation studies as in other approaches. Methods used for reliability include inter-observer agreement, respondent stability coefficient measurements and inter-investigator agreement. Methods available for assessing validity include:

- checking with other observers which behaviours should be associated with which categories
- conducting a cluster analysis by using a schedule and comparing this with a (qualitative) mini-case study description
- using two different observation schedules that possess the same focus.

OTHER FORMS OF DATA COLLECTION

Content analysis

Content analysis is a common term for different types of textual analysis, whose approaches emphasize either quantitative and/or qualitative descriptions and analysis of documents of various types – official, semi-official and unofficial. Content analyses are a very useful approach, particularly for the researcher who is looking at a historical or political issue. Documents may contain valuable information in their own right, but additionally they throw light upon contemporary ideologies, belief systems and commonly held views.

Essentially, there are three types of document:

1. *Primary sources*, written at the time of the event; these may be official communications, journals, newspaper articles, minutes of meetings, reports, letters, commentaries, etc
2. *Secondary sources*, written some time after the event, involving commentaries on situations and events (eg newspaper editorials)
3. *Statistical sources* (eg census and contemporary surveys).

Documents may relate to historical or contemporary interests.

Scott (1990) has provided a checklist against which such sources should be evaluated.

1. Authenticity – is the origin of the document certain?
2. Credibility – is the evidence biased towards a particular viewpoint?
3. Representativeness – is the document typical of similar documents of that period? (If the research topic is a historical one a problem can arise over the selective survival of documents.)
4. Meaning – is the researcher absolutely clear about the meaning of the document?

When conducting content and/or historical research the first step is to find and access the document. This is particularly important if the document is rare. It is not normal for such documents to be allowed out of a library, archive or government department in which they are stored. The document will have to be read *in situ*, often with notes to be taken in pencil only. If it is intended to study documents of great age then it might be necessary to use gloves to handle them. A magnifying glass is particularly useful for handwritten documents. Photocopies of older materials are often not allowed, especially where the binding may be suspect.

It is important to note not only the content but who is making the statements (do they have particular views or interests?) and what were the reasons for why things were as they were?

Diaries

Diaries are another very useful form of data collection as well as being materials for content analysis. Diaries can be used in a variety of ways and in connection with a range of different methodological approaches. They are also useful in supplementing information obtainable from other sources and in helping to improve the validity of that data by means of 'triangulation'.

Areas where diaries have been employed are:

■ ethnographic studies
■ action research studies
■ case studies of institutions.

There are various ways of keeping a diary, but many researchers feel happier if the material is structured in some way. One way of imposing a structure upon diaries, if this is required, is to identify 'critical incidents' in fieldwork. This is based partly on the assumption that life is about making decisions and that these revolve around particular critical incidents, and it is the documentation of these that provides the 'essential' data. Both Bell (1993) and Tripp (1993) give full details of how to use diaries.

Accounts and biographical research

Accounts and biographical research are methods of data collection not unrelated to the use of diaries, except that often these accounts are elicited as a result of a conversational and/or unstructured interview approach (Cohen and Manion, 1994). It is also possible to use accounts in a piece of qualitative research, and to quantify some of the data using discourse analysis methods.

Data collection methods such as interviewing, use of diaries and accounts are also useful in a type of methodology known as the 'thick description'. This is one method of coping with the enormous amount of information available to be recorded during an ethnographic study. Essentially, a central figure in the situation is identified (eg the class teacher), who will be involved in a number of activities that will involve a number of other significant individuals. The data collection processes therefore involve looking at the interactions that the central character (the teacher) has with other individuals in the room (ie pupils, helpers, etc). Data collecting techniques such as diaries, accounts and observations are all possible here. Thick description has been used to identify good practice in the Teaching of English to Speakers of Other Languages (TESOL) (Moreland *et al.*, 1998) in order to transfer that practice to different contexts and situations.

Protocol analysis

More focused, however is the use of protocol analysis. This technique aims to discover thinking processes by the use of articulated statements by the respondent. Ericsson and Simon (1993) describe it in these terms:

> One means frequently used to gain information about the course of the cognitive processes is to probe the subjects' internal states by verbal methods. (p1)

This technique has been used, for instance, to discover how subjects with different linguistic backgrounds are able to make sense of examination questions and interpret the requirements of the question in order to formulate their answer. It has also been used to research problem-solving strategies used by students and practitioners.

Tests and testing

Tests and testing techniques can have a role in research. The tests might be official tests of knowledge, understanding and application, such as National Curriculum Standard Attainment Targets (SATs), or be skill-based assessments, as in many vocational qualifications. Such tests, with their statistical reliability, are quite common and often available 'off the shelf'.

Tests can also have a psychological emphasis. They may be tests of ability (intellectual, spatial, learning style, etc), achievement, or of aspects of personality (eg introversion/extroversion). Where there is no test available for the specific attribute or population under investigation it may be necessary to devise or adapt a test.

Existing and bespoke tests are dealt with in the standard texts such as those by Guilford (1954), Anastasi (1988) or Kline (1993). It is essential that such tests satisfy the usual validity and reliability criteria and that, if they are commercial tests, they have been standardized on a similar population to that being studied (in terms of age, ability, social class, etc).

If it is felt that such tests are relevant it is most important that the researcher becomes familiar with the test, what it is measuring and what the results mean. Some commercial test publishers require that the researcher has appropriate qualifications or has undergone suitable training before they will issue the test. Anyone contemplating the use of such tests should study Jackson (1996), where such matters are discussed in greater detail. Levy and Goldstein (1984) provide a list of common tests used in education and training in the UK, as does the National Foundation for Educational Research (NFER). A more comprehensive listing, with the emphasis on tests developed in the USA, is that by Buros (1978).

Repertory grid research

A repertory grid is the set of bipolar concepts an individual has that form the framework of their analysis and evaluation of situations, events and people. Such constructs are considered to be relatively stable and relate to personality. In repertory grid analysis respondents are asked to compare items (eg people) to identify which qualities form a bipolar scale (Good—Bad, Hot—Cold, etc). Fransella and Bannister (1977) describe the technique, and an example of its use is given in Olson and Reid (1982).

Sociometry

Sociometry is a method of obtaining and then representing the structure and relationships among a group of individuals diagrammatically. A research sample might be a class of children or a group of managers. The data for constructing the sociogram is drawn from interviews or observations with the individuals who make up the group.

The technique is often used to identify potential leaders (stars) and those individuals who have largely been rejected by the rest of the group (isolates), and is a fairly easy technique to use with small groups. For larger groups the construction of the network diagrams can be a daunting task. Scott (1991) has suggested alternative techniques by which these difficulties can be overcome (see also the section on multi-dimensional scaling in the next chapter).

EQUIPMENT

For much of the work described above the routine equipment of stationery, notebooks, fax, telephone, word processing and photocopying facilities are all that is required. For some studies more sophisticated technology may be needed. Observation studies may require a still camera and/or a video-recorder. Often the researcher may need to tape-record interviews, particularly with younger children who are not distracted by the equipment. If the respondents move around a radio microphone in conjunction with a tape-recorder may be required. Finally, some testing procedures require quite complex apparatus to be used in conjunction with a test.

CONCLUSION

What this chapter has sought to provide is an overview of the variety of techniques available to the researcher. In all cases the choice of data collection techniques should be on the basis of 'sufficient unto the task'. That is a tall order, but one well worth achieving.

5

The Presentation and Analysis of Data

THE THREE ASPECTS OF DATA ANALYSIS

Data analysis, along with data collection, is the real essence of the research process. Data should be used to the full but not gone beyond, for to do so is to make unwarranted claims. For instance, conclusions made on the basis of data collected on the mathematical abilities of a group of inner-city children in the UK may well apply to a similar group of rural children in the UK, or to a group of inner-city children in the USA, but this cannot be assumed. There is always a sense in which results are provisional – it cannot be assumed that the findings will automatically apply to whole populations or through time, though sampling techniques may make the inferences into probabilities rather than possibilities. As a piece of research may well have started with some premises derived from a literature survey, and embodied in a series of research questions, the data analysis should be carried out in a way that allows for the data to be linked directly to a consideration of those premises.

In any research project in the social sciences data will be collected and be available in a variety of forms. Three tasks at least confront the researcher in dealing with data: coding, presentation and analysis of the data.

Coding is the process of structuring data into an analysable form. The data will also need to be collated and presented in a way that makes it understandable and interesting to the researcher and subsequent readers. The researcher will need the data to be presented in a clear and concise manner. Statistical data, for instance, could be presented as:

- a table
- a graph
- a pie chart.

On the other hand, if qualitative data (eg interview data) has been collected it, too, needs to be clearly presented. Tape-recorded data, for instance, needs to be available for analysis by others (see the section on reliability in Chapter 4) by being converted into transcripts. Typically, respondents are identified by coding letters or numbers that allow cross-referencing but retain anonymity. Characteristics (age band, gender, socio-economic group, position in the organization, etc) can still be identified.

Finally, the data needs to be analysed. The data is sorted into broader themes and outcomes and related to the research questions, literature survey outcomes and theories and/or models that have been projected.

Analysis can be time consuming. Often a researcher may have a very clear idea of possible outcomes, as common sense or pilot studies will have presented possibilities. If this is the case it is possible that an initial scheme of analysis will have been prepared. In other cases the method(s) of analysis can only be decided on and used when the full scope of the data is apparent, as often happens with qualitative data.

CODING DATA

This technique is important for both quantitative and qualitative data. The purpose of coding is to render the data into a form in which it can be presented and analysed. It can also serve the important but subsidiary function of identifying any important and significant trends that may be present. That is, coding allows the researcher to get to know their data.

Coding of quantitative data

Typically, coding of quantitative data uses either letters, numerals or alpha-numeric (a mixture of both letters and numbers) codes to describe the data, which thus becomes capable of being analysed without reference to each of the responses of the sample. It is important to code non-responses as well as responses, for a non-response is itself a form of response and data. The following example demonstrates coding using letters and numbers.

Suppose the following question appeared on a questionnaire:

Question: In which of the following areas do you feel that you require some staff development activity?

Managing resources	YES [ ]	NO [ ]
Managing personnel	YES [ ]	NO [ ]
Selection of personnel	YES [ ]	NO [ ]
Programme development	YES [ ]	NO [ ]
Subject content	YES [ ]	NO [ ]
None of the above	YES [ ]	NO [ ]

The resultant coding might look, initially, as follows (including non-responses):

	Man res	Man staff	Selecn	Prog dev	Subj content	None
Respondent 1	Y	Y	N	N	N	NR
Respondent 2	N	N	N	Y	Y	NR
Respondent 3	N	N	Y	N	N	NR

If a numeric coding approach was used, it might look like this:

Item	20	21	22	23	24	25
Respondent 1	1	1	2	2	2	0
Respondent 2	2	2	2	1	1	0
Respondent 3	2	2	1	2	2	0

The results are now ready to be transferred to a computer-based spreadsheet (such as Excel) where they can be analysed using one of the standard computer-based packages. Alternatively, the researcher may prefer to conduct the analysis 'long hand' – especially if they have an aversion to modern technology.

Just a glance at the above results will reveal a trend that may well be worth following up, as the respondents (admittedly from a sample of just three!) seem to fall into two categories – those who require subject-specific skills related to content and course planning and those who require managerial skills. No conclusions can, of course, be based on such a small sample, but there might be something here worth following up.

Coding qualitative data

Coding qualitative data is often more difficult to do, for the process is essentially one of identifying 'chunks' of data (a sentence, an episode or critical incident) and initially giving it a descriptive label. Strauss and Corbin (1989) are particularly valuable here. They use the concepts of 'open', 'axial' and 'selective' coding to identify the different types that can occur. The initial 'chunking' and appellation of a descriptive label is what Strauss and Corbin call 'open coding':

> The process of breaking down, examining, comparing, conceptualizing and categorizing data. (p61)

The other types of coding are dealt with below under analysis, for they are more discerning coding approaches that seek to refine and re-examine the initial descriptors given in open coding.

ACTIVITY

Construct a plan for a piece of small-scale research.

Include about three research questions.

Devise two data collecting instruments, one of which will be used to collect quantitative data and the other to collect qualitative data.

Make some *preliminary* suggestions about what methods of analysis could be used in each case.

ANALYSING DATA

Simple quantitative data analysis

It is not the intention of this book to convert its readers into statisticians, nor to be a statistical text, but there are a number of statistical data analysis techniques with which researchers in the social sciences ought to be familiar. There are at least two ways that researchers can draw conclusions from quantitative data. First, the data may be used to describe the situation using descriptive statistics. This might involve using pie charts, tables or graphs. Second, the researcher may wish to *infer* something about the much wider population from which that sample was drawn. In this case one would require the help of inferential statistics.

If the objective of the research is to carry out the latter type of analysis then it is essential that the form of the data to be collected is decided, along with the inferential statistical tests to be used, before the research is commenced. There are some types of data for which there are no easily usable statistical tests. In order to do this some basic ideas need to be introduced.

Types of quantitative data

Figure 5.1 illustrates the various types of data that could be obtained in a piece of research.

The term nominal refers to data such as make of car, gender, school attended, where a number is being used as a label and no notion of quantity is intended. If a question asks a respondent to identify the make of car that they drive, a Ford might be given the label '1' while a Renault might be given the label '2'.

Quantity data, on the other hand, is data that does measure an amount of something. It may be discontinuous (occurs in whole numbers, eg a family size of 4.25 would be meaningless in this context) or continuous data, which accepts unbroken ranges within items such as age (12.5 years) or scores in achievement tests.

Ordinal data is ranked in some way. For instance, respondents may be asked to place preferences in rank order or use a Likert scale (eg 'strongly agree', 'agree', 'neutral', 'disagree', 'strongly disagree').

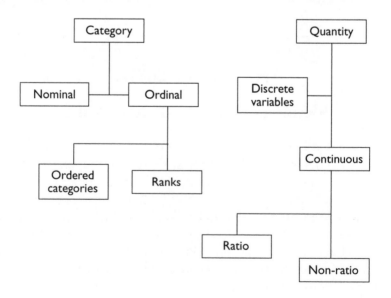

Figure 5.1 *Types of research data*

Finally, 'ratio' and 'non-ratio' data need to be defined. Ratio data occurs when the data is related directly to, and compared with, a baseline value. Height, for instance, is usually measured in feet or in metres starting from zero, while the absolute scale of temperature commences at 0K (–273° Celsius). On the other hand, non-ratio measures used in the social sciences tend to be expressed with respect to a norm rather than an absolute value. This gives a ratio value as, for example, when it is stated that someone has a verbal reasoning score of 121, the average for a given population being 100.

Variability within samples and populations

If a particular attribute is being measured it is most unlikely that every member of a sample or, indeed, every member of the population will possess that attribute in exactly the same amount. All will not be exactly the same height, the same weight, have the same ability in mathematics or the same attitude towards equal opportunities training. There will be a degree of variability among the various members of the group.

The normal distribution curve

If a random sample has been selected then this variability often follows a slope called a normal distribution curve. If this (a 'bell'-shaped curve) is the case (and there are statistical tests that can be applied to confirm this), a number of predictions can made about the sample. Powerful tests using inferential statistics can be used to infer things about the population from which the sample was drawn. Such data is usually known as parametric data, though the actual definition of the term parametric in statistics is more precise than this. Where the sample does not follow a normal distribution curve (eg the data was presented in ranks rather than in quantities, or came from a population that was non-random or skewed), the data is called non-parametric and different statistical tests are required.

If the data lies on a normal distribution curve much useful information can be derived. A key statistic is the standard deviation (SD), which provides a measure of the spread of the data from the mean. For a normal distribution curve 68 per cent of the population will lie +/– 1 SD from the mean and approximately 95 per cent of the population will lie +/– 2× SD of the mean. By way of an example, suppose that science and English tests are given to a group of students. When calculated, the mean score in science is 60 and 65 in English. In science, let it be supposed that the standard deviation is 15 as against 5 in English. Bill (one of the students) scored 90 in science while Laura (another student) scored 80 in English. How would we rate Bill's performance in science with Laura's in English?

Given the standard deviations, Laura has provided the better performance. Her score of 80 in English has placed her 15 points above the mean. This is equivalent to 3.0 SD (80–65 divided by 5). In effect, her score is exceeded by only 0.15 per cent of her group. On the other hand Bill's score of 90 in science places him 30 points above the mean, ie 2.0 SD. Bill's score will be exceeded by 2.5 per cent of his group. Using the normal curve of distribution in such cases enables the researcher to standardize results from different tests against each other.

Inferential statistical tests

A range of inferential statistical tests are available, provided the researcher is sure about what they wish to measure and compare; and the type of data they have.

Many of the standard books on statistics explain how inferential statistical tests can be completed using a calculator. Most of the tests are also available in the standard computer packages such as Minitab, SPSS and SAS. Since these packages can make life easier for the researcher it is advisable to check the facilities available before commencing data analysis. Figure 5.2 provides details of some of the more commonly used tests.

Figure 5.2 should not be taken as comprehensive, for other (less common) tests such as analysis of variance are also available. Statistical tests are available for a wide range of eventualities, but the most common are tests of difference, correlations and contingency table analysis.

Tests of difference These tests are used where it is suspected that groups differ significantly on or as a result of a particular variable. The groups might have been subjected to differing treatments on that variable, ie they may be similar in all respects other than that they have received two different treatments (eg been taught differently). One might wish to evaluate, for instance, two different methods of training electronics technicians in basic circuit analysis. Two groups might be taken that are similar in all respects (matched), except that each experiences a different training method. The two groups would then be tested at the conclusion of their training. The test results are compared using an appropriate statistical test selected from Figure 5.2.

Correlations Correlations (a mutual connection) can be used if it is suspected that there may be a relationship between two or more

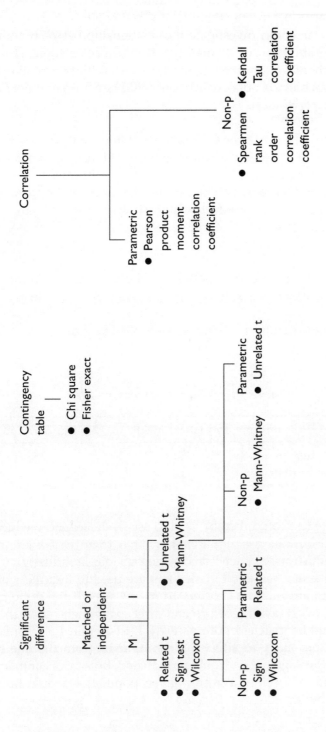

Figure 5.2 *Some basic inferential statistical tests*

variables within a group. It must be remembered that correlations do not necessarily mean that there is a causal connection between the variables. One could investigate the relationship between ability in science and ability in mathematics and find a correlation. This may mean that there is a causal relationship between ability in mathematics and ability in science, but equally there could be a third or other factors causing the correlation.

Contingency table analysis Contingency table analysis assists the researcher in determining whether an observed distribution is significant. Contingency tables can be used to help with the processing of questionnaire data by collating data in tabular form. Supposing one wishes to know about the effects of industrial experience on the subsequent uptake by students of industrial careers, one might ask about the effects of groups that:

1. received (or did not) industrial experience in their training and
2. subsequently embarked (or did not) on a career in industry.

The responses from the individuals could then be grouped in a contingency table such as shown in Table 5.1.

Table 5.1 *Sample contingency table*

	Industrial input	No industrial input
Career in industry	26	28
No career in industry	31	07

A chi square test could then be used to assess the extent to which the above distributions are significant (ie that there is a relationship between industrial experience and taking up jobs in industry).

The terms matched and independent are used to indicate whether the two samples might be correlated in any way. If the same group was tested twice (as in a before and after experiment) then the two groups could be matched. Alternatively, if two groups are similar on every variable likely to affect the result, apart from the one being examined, then again they would be matched. By way of contrast, two groups randomly selected from a given population would be independent samples.

Significance

The term significance is frequently used in connection with inferential statistics. It can never be said in social science that a supposed difference between two sets of figures is absolutely significant – all one can express is the probability of this difference occurring other than by random chance. For instance, if a coin is tossed into the air 20 times and on nine occasions it is tails whereas on 11 occasions it is heads we would probably not think that anything was seriously amiss. However, if there were 19 heads and only one tail then we might suspect that something significant was operating.

To quantify these relationships probability levels of 5 per cent or 1 per cent are normally applied. This means that the chance of the differences between two groups occurring entirely by chance are one in 20 and one in 100 respectively. Tests that advise the level and direction of significance are called one-tailed and two-tailed tests.

One-tailed and two-tailed tests

In addition to providing an indication of the degree of significance between two variables, one-tailed and two-tailed tests provide indications of the direction (positive or negative/inverse) of the relationship. By way of example, let us assume a null hypothesis is developed that there is:

> no difference in score in agricultural science between rural and urban children.

The presence of a significant difference between the two groups could mean that either the urban children have performed better than the rural children or the rural children have performed better than the urban children. Where the direction of the relationship is not as important as the significance of a relationship, a two-tailed test is used.

If the research question is reformulated as rural children being expected to perform better at a subject such as agricultural science than urban children by virtue of their environment, the resultant test would be a one-tailed test, for the hypothesis posits not only a significant difference but also a direction for that difference.

Other statistical tests

There are a number of other, more specialized tests that have not been discussed here (eg ANOVA, Kendall coefficient of concordance), as their use is less common. The researcher should refer to one of the standard books on statistics for these and the conditions under which they should be used. Since some of these methods are quite complex access to one of the standard computer packages and the associated manuals is necessary.

In summary, the questions that need to be asked about statistical tests in quantitative data analysis are:

1. What sort of data has been obtained?
2. Is the data:
   - parametric?
   - non-parametric?
3. Which of the following is being sought
   - significant differences
   - correlations
   - contingency table analysis?
4. What level of significance is required?
5. Is the test to operate under one-tailed or two-tailed conditions?
6. Are the subjects:
   - matched/repeated measures
   - independent?

Complex quantitative data analysis

In quantitative data analysis there remain a raft of statistical approaches that go beyond simple tests. If the researcher thinks such approaches might be applicable to them it is often beneficial to carry out exploratory data analysis.

Exploratory data analysis

Exploratory data analysis is a preliminary examination of data undertaken in order to ascertain if there are any patterns in the data that warrant a more detailed examination with more specialist techniques. Marsh (1988) suggests a number of methods of performing this task. One of the easier methods is the 'stem and leaf plot', a means of looking at the general shape of the data.

An example of such a plot is given in Figure 5.3, where the test scores of 15 individuals are presented. The overall shape of these scores was not obvious initially, so the scores have been rearranged using categories ten units long. Thus, the score of individual 1 falls within the category 7, as does any score between 70 and 79. Similarly the seven

Individual	1	2	3	4	5	6	7	8	9	10	11	12	13	14	15
Score	71	72	81	84	66	61	63	90	31	65	68	54	60	61	79

A stem and leaf plot

Score category   Individual sample members

```
3 | 1
4 |
5 | 4
6 | 0 1 1 6 3 5 8
7 | 1 2 9
8 | 1 4
9 | 0
```

Figure 5.3 *Example of a stem and leaf plot*

individuals with scores in the range 60–69 are placed in category 6. These new category scores are then represented using the ten unit categories. This gives the lower stem and leaf plot, which clearly shows the form of the data in a broad sense.

ACTIVITY

Collect some quantitative data from friends, family or fellow students. The data should be simple quantity data and non-controversial, eg distance from home to work, size of family, number of pets. Ensure that there are at least ten respondents in your sample.

1. Plot out the data to see if you have a bell-shaped curve.
2. Try a χ^2 (chi square) 'goodness-of-fit' test to see if the data is normally distributed.
3. Try a 'stem and leaf plot' as an alternative to looking at the general 'shape' of the data.

Cluster analysis

This is a computer-based method which groups individuals on the basis of measured characteristics. It might well be that one can identify common characteristics of a group enrolling for an evening class (by address, age, gender, socio-economic group, level of education, ethnicity, etc). Cluster analysis techniques are often used in market research. Everett (1980) discusses this technique and provides some examples of its use.

Factor analysis

Factor analysis seeks to describe a range of variables (eg questionnaire responses) in terms of a more basic set of underlying factors. This technique is used often with responses derived using a Likert scale. Were one attempting to measure attitudes to industry one might develop a set of statements such as those below.

1. In industry you are dependent on colleagues for success.
2. An important part of an industrial career is managing other people.
3. You need to have been to university to succeed in industry.
4. Industry is about doing things to help the community.
5. Working in industry requires 'flair' more than anything else.
6. People who work in industry are very intelligent.
7. Industry is not the place for the less able.
8. The advice of parents is important in selecting a job in industry.
9. Most of my friends wish to work in industry.

Respondents would be invited to strongly agree/agree/disagree/strongly disagree with each of the statements. The results are then subjected to a factor analysis, the responses to which might reveal that the answers to statements (1) (2) (8) and (9) correlate with each other, suggesting a 'social/interpersonal relationship' factor. Similarly, statements (3), (6) and (7) correlate, suggesting a 'cognitive/intellectual' factor; while (4) and (5) correlate, implying a 'creative/problem-solving' factor. Such scales and factors typically will lead to additional validation trials and the rewriting of items to produce a greater degree of discrimination between them.

Principal components analysis is a more sophisticated form of factor analysis. To use this technique it is necessary to have access to a computer software package such as SPSS, where the manual will provide all the necessary help. Kline (1994) and Child (1990) explain how the method works.

Discriminant analysis

Discriminant analysis seeks to link a number of possible outcomes statistically to variables that appear to be related to these outcomes. One might be investigating the role of various study skills in enabling students to achieve success in their A level examinations; related factors might be the amount of time the students spent revising, the holding of part-time jobs, etc. Using discriminant analysis these variables could then be related to success or failure in the examinations. Klecka (1980) deals with this technique in more detail.

Regression methods

This is where an outcome (dependent variable) is related to various independent variables that are weighted to show their relative importance. Regression methods take a variety of forms and are useful in modelling social processes.

Path analysis

Path analysis is a method of assessing the extent to which a correlation between two or more variables is a causal relationship. It is commonly used in association with the more sophisticated correlation methods.

Multidimensional scaling

If one has measured the proximity (correlation) of different items it is possible to produce a graphical display to represent these proximities pictorially. These items could be:

- variables such as achievement or ability
- individuals in a group relationship such as one might obtain from a sociometric study
- items on a questionnaire or attitude scale.

Kruskal and Wish (1978) and Scott (1991) cover this technique in more detail.

Correlation methods

Some of the simpler forms of correlation have already been discussed. There are other, more specialist correlational tests and techniques such as:

Data	Technique
Continuous/continuous and parametric	Pearson product moment
Rank/rank	Spearman rank order
Rank/rank	Kendall test
Artificial dichotomy/continuous	Biserial r
True dichotomy/continuous	Point biserial r
True dichotomy/True dichotomy	Phi
Artificial dichotomy/Artificial dichotomy	Tetrachoric

In addition there are:

- partial correlation coefficients (variable one vs variable two with a third, confounding variable controlled for)
- canonical correlation coefficients (a set of variables vs a set of variables)
- multiple correlation coefficients (set of independent variables vs one dependent variable).

Multilevel modelling

This is a technique developed largely at the University of London Institute of Education, in which the various levels of factors can be taken into account using statistical methods.

Follow-up references

This discussion of quantitative methods of analysis has only given the briefest introduction to the subject. Greene and D'Oliveira (1982) and Wright (1997) give a more extensive overview of basic statistical methods; while Guilford and Fruchter (1979) and Blalock (1981) provide more in-depth treatment.

Siegel (1956) and Kendall (1970) are very good for non-parametric methods. For the more specialist techniques it is helpful to consult books in the Sage series on quantitative methods and/or the manuals for the various software packages such as Minitab and SPSS.

Methods of analysing qualitative data

The analysis of qualitative data does not present the same neat and predictable patterns typically presented by quantitative data. Qualitative data is much richer and more diverse and therefore amenable to a range of analyses which may at times appear to conflict with one other. Nonetheless, all qualitative data require there to be coding of either a descriptive (what is this an example of?) or categorical type (this is an example of . . .). .

Content analysis

Content analysis is a method of analysing qualitative data that almost converts it back into quantitative data. It is thus not a technique universally admired among researchers committed to the qualitative paradigm.

To demonstrate an example of content analysis, consider the following 'raw data' provided by a teacher and a salesperson, who were asked briefly to describe their jobs.

The teacher

Work begins at about eight o'clock. The day usually begins with a school assembly. This enables all of the pupils to meet together. It gives them a sense of belonging to one organization. After all, for the rest of the day they are in tutor groups, subject groups, etc.

After assembly all classes then go to their classrooms. Pupils in this school are 'set' in mathematics only, so that you can imagine how difficult and chaotic the whole organization becomes. I'm sure that more time is spent on organization and management methods than on teaching the subject.

Lunch hour lasts from twelve until one, and all sixth form classes have a sports afternoon on Wednesdays.

By and large, the content of what we teach is very much determined by the National Curriculum and examination board requirements, although there is flexibility, particularly with respect to teaching methods and order of presentation.

The salesman

I have found that the current motor car that I am trying to sell is very unreliable – in fact I would like to move to a dealer who holds better quality machines.

I have, therefore, to be very persuasive to get the public to buy the car, otherwise I don't sell any and my salary is much reduced. You can imagine how popular that makes me at home.

My family usually expects a holiday overseas every year and instability in one's income can be very problematic. I think that I shall most certainly leave my current post within the next three years.

This is one of the problems in working in the motor trade, those of us employed in sales find it can be very difficult to plan very far ahead.

There are a number of ways one might begin to analyse this data. One way is to use content analysis (counting factors considered significant). One might analyse the texts on the basis of the extent to which each passage represents an egocentric (not using the word pejoratively) orientation. So one might count the number of such words ('I', 'we', 'us' and 'our') in order to have some point of comparison between the two passages. There are, of course, other bases on which one can compare them. The use of content analysis is a systematic procedure using the following stages.

1. Select representative samples of text.
2. Select appropriate categories; these may be phrases, words or 'units of meaning' or amounts of text which define an issue, ie racism, sexism, egocentricity, individual or organizational goals.
3. Select appropriate recording units; these may be:
    -   single words, eg 'I', 'We', 'Us'
    -   themes, eg an ideology, developing world, technology, language
    -   a characteristic, eg 'working class', teacher of technical subjects
    -   a particular topic or idiom.
4. The context in which the text was produced needs to be known.
5. Select suitable enumeration systems (key words, frequency, space used, intensity of statements, and apply them (count or measure).

The results can be tabulated, presented graphically and analysed for regularities and/or balance or absence of items.

A more advanced example of content analysis using visual mapping and representation of data is provided by Paulston (1997).

Methods based on categorization

In many respects these are probably the most valuable ways of analysing the data, by constructing and using an analytical framework. This can be either an open coding approach, using (either literally or metaphorically) the 'scissors and paste' method, or a categorical approach, where preconstructed categories (axial codes) are placed over the data or used as a sieve to bring out key aspects. In the former approach the text is analysed descriptively, with few preconceived notions. Various categories may be tried on the data for their relevance, such as:

■   Primary/elementary teachers vs Secondary/high school teachers
■   Managerial staff vs Non-managerial staff

- Blue-collar vs White-collar staff
- Science and technology teachers vs Arts and humanities teachers.

The researcher describes or names significant blocks of data (segments of interviews, observations and so on) and then moves meaningful segments of the text around until patterns start to emerge and cross-tabulations start to make sense. As more data is inserted into the matrix existing patterns may be reinforced or modified.

In such processes it is useful to have a fellow researcher or colleague at hand who can validate and confirm the categorization used (ie analyse the data and arrive at the same or similar conclusions). Alternatively, when patterns start to emerge, the researcher might wish to return to the institution from which the data was derived to confirm the interpretation made first hand with the respondents.

If the analysis has to be conducted manually (without a computer) one way of managing this process is to record interview statements on paper. Photocopies are made of these sheets which are then are cut up and sorted into piles or taped to a large piece of paper holding similar responses. On the back of each piece a note is made locating the origin of that piece of text, often in shorthand (eg Sec/man/exp might indicate a teacher in a secondary school who is experienced and who has management responsibilities). Alternatively a code number and/or letter might suffice. One then continues to sort the text segments until patterns emerge. Once completed the data is represented in analytical format to aid further discussion and argument.

Network methods

Network data analysis methods construct a network of processes and relationships from the text data. This approach is particularly useful in the analysis of verbal protocols (streams of explanation). To carry out this method the researcher first categorizes the text, identifying any networks of regular patterns of response or activity. In researching problem-solving approaches, for instance, the researcher might observe a respondent needing to import information to solve a problem and then carrying out a calculation using that information. These two forms of action could be referred to as execution operations. The respondent might then check their work for faults, review their work so far and plan their next task. These are defined as monitoring operations, necessary as action proceeds. On this basis one can construct a network of categories of action. Networks produced in this way could be compared to find out the following.

■ What relationship is there between problem-solving strategy and outcome?

■ What is the relative frequency of control and execution operations?

■ Is there any relationship between the form of problem (eg the 'closed' type of problem often encountered in mathematics, physics and chemistry and the more 'open' type of problem encountered in biology and engineering) and the different operations performed?

■ What type of strategies do respondents employ (linear, cyclic repetitive, etc)?

■ Does that make a difference where the first language of the respondent is different from the language in which the problem is framed?

Network methods are described in full by Bliss *et al.* (1983) and are also referred to in Cohen and Manion (1994).

Ethnographic data analysis

If the object of the analysis is to generate grounded theory (research that interrelates theory with practical situational observation and understanding), we return to Strauss and Corbin (1989) and their use of 'open', 'axial' and 'selective' coding. Open coding was referred to in the section on Coding (see p61). This is followed by axial coding, which is defined as:

A set of procedures whereby data are put back together in new ways after open coding, by making connections between categories. (p96)

The final part of the process is selective coding, which is:

The process of selecting the core category, systematically relating it to other categories, validating those relationships, and filling in categories that require further refinement and development. (p116)

Researchers use such analytical devices in different ways. Thus it is often a useful exercise to examine articles by well-known ethnographers to review their own unique approach to ethnographic analysis.

ACTIVITY

Devise a simple interview schedule containing about 8–10 questions that seek to establish a respondent's preferred subjects at secondary school.

Carry out the interview on about four of your friends and then code your answers to check if any patterns start to emerge.

Miscellaneous methods

Many of the following methods will be specific to particular data research concerns.

Career paths

Life histories can be a valuable way of making sense of the lives of individuals. There are various ways of analysing the data. Hatch and Wisniewski (1995) view the biography as a story:

> Narrative analysis relates events and actions to one another by configuring them as contributors to the advancement of a plot . . . The result of a narrative analysis is an explanation that is retrospective, having linked past events together to account for how a final outcome might have come about. In this analysis, the researcher attends to the temporal and unfolding dimension of human experience by organizing the events of the data along a before-after continuum. (p16)

With a larger sample it is possible to construct a lifeline diagram for a group, illustrating the various paths that have been taken and the complexity of the decisions forced on certain groups.

Semantic net systems

The work of Leinhardt (1993) provides an excellent example of this methodology in practice. The author was interested in the various approaches used to present explanations in a course on a specific aspect of US history. Lessons were video-taped, the data characterized and the resulting sets of explanatory devices were presented as semantic nets. One net or set of connections is illustrated in Figure 5.4.

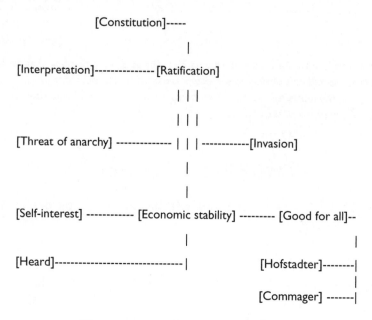

Figure 5.4 *Example of semantic net*

Discourse analysis

Many forms of observational study take some account of the amount and form of discourse occurring within a social setting, but in some cases it may be desirable to venture further into this area. Introductory texts by Stubbs (1983) and Coulthard (1985) are worthwhile, while the studies by Sinclair and Coulthard (1975) and Edwards and Westgate (1994) provide examples of the practical applications of these techniques. The latter, in particular, is an excellent guide to the study and interpretation of classroom talk.

ACTIVITY

Select two different types of articles from a journal, perhaps one with a quantitative emphasis and one with a more qualitative emphasis.

1. Read the articles and establish how the data has been analysed. What methods have been used?
2. What are the advantages of the methods used?
3. What alternative methods might you have used to analyse the data?

Researchers will find it of great value to refer to the excellent texts Dey (1993) and Miles and Huberman (1994) on qualitative data analysis

CONCLUSION

Data analysis is a central part of the research process. Luckily researchers have available a panoply of approaches and techniques for carrying out data analysis. Deciding which are the best and most suitable for any particular research project is a tricky activity, but careful thought and consideration early on will repay the researcher later on. It is a safe bet that any researcher will continue to learn from data analysis experiences, if only to make sure that they do it better next time.

6

Using Literature Sources

INTRODUCTION AND OVERVIEW

A key aspect of almost all research projects is the completion of a literature review. Saying it that way makes it seem simple, which is often less the case the further up the education system you go. Typically, however, a literature review involves or assists the achievement of four things. First, as the words imply, a literature review is a critical analysis of the existing literature on your proposed research subject. Second, carrying out a literature review can be a significant help in the process of clarifying and framing research questions as you find out what has been done (and not done) prior to your research. Third, an often hidden aspect of the literature review is a comparative account of the suitability, advantages and disadvantages of the particular research methodologies that were chosen in the past and are currently being considered in order to research a particular topic. In many ways, therefore, a literature review is an important 'ground-clearing' exercise during a research project.

The first two aspects – a review of the literature that deals with the proposed research subject – are normally contained in a literature review. The third aspect – the choice of the research approach and particular methodology – typically forms part of a research methodology chapter, where the attempt is made to explain and justify the research approach and particular techniques applied in the research. Fourth, and finally, once the research has been carried out, the literature is re-engaged with, as it is normal to refer back to the literature when discussing research findings, and how they relate to (extend/differ/modify) the existing relevant literature.

This chapter deals with the first aspect only. That is, it is limited to the literature review of the subject or focus of the research to be carried out.

ACTIVITY

1. Consider any research that you have either carried out or have read about and give yourself marks out of ten (ten being perfect) for the extent to which the four aspects of literature were dealt with.
2. What (if anything) does that tell you about the quality of the research and the research report/thesis, and what is needed for the current research being planned?

WHAT DOES IT MEAN TO CARRY OUT A REVIEW?

Before starting a literature review it is useful to analyse what the word 'review' actually means. The activity below will help with this analysis.

ACTIVITY

Reflect upon the word 'review' and write down what the word means to you as a researcher. Try to use individual words rather than sentences!

Be clear what carrying out a literature review means. Clues to this are provided by the following thesaurus of the word 'review'. Read through the list and consider the meaning of each word. Roll each word around and define it for yourself. Add to your list of words in the activity above as necessary.

A thesaurus of 'review' (as in literature review)

- Analysis
- Discussion
- Judgement
- Round up
- Theme
- Breakdown
- Exploration
- Perusal
- Study
- Writing
- Criticism
- Investigation
- Recount
- Summary

If you added to your list of words you will have seen that the word review has three aspects to it.

First, to review means to peruse or provide a round up. This implies that a literature review should be:

- comprehensive (cover as much of the literature as possible)
- relevant (the review should not be concerned to discuss research simply because you have read it and do not want to waste it, found it interesting, or solely to display your analytical capacities).

In some cases it is necessary to rework the literature (develop a different perspective on it) so as to relate to your concerns.

Second, a literature review should involve critical study and investigation. This implies that it:

- be an accurate account of each separate piece of literature, noting its good and bad features, and particularly its relevance to the research concerns that have been identified
- compare and contrast the different books and articles, both with each other and with your own perspectives on your topic of investigation
- involve judgements of the literature, mainly in terms of your own concerns and needs.

Third, a literature review should aim to be a comprehensive summary of the relevant literature. This implies that it should:

- be focused (not be allowed to side-track you from the main issues)
- be inclined to pithiness (be brief while attempting to draw out the main themes and issues as they relate to your research)
- provide a round up of literature with some connection to your own research
- clearly identify any literature that may have been relevant but could not be obtained during the completion of the research process.

TIP

Identify what is the focus or foci (if there is more than one) of your own research, and use that to help you determine what it is that you read. Do not allow yourself to get side-tracked, as time is often short and deadlines *have to be met!*

WHERE IN A RESEARCH PROJECT IS A LITERATURE REVIEW NECESSARY?

ACTIVITY

Take the opportunity to have a look at or reflect on research such as an MPhil or PhD thesis relevant to your identified research concerns. In reviewing the thesis identify and note down those places where there is clearly a discussion of the literature as a major focus of the text.

Typically there are three places in a research project where some review of relevant literature is required. These are when a researcher is:

1. considering what has already been researched and written about the topic(s) or research question(s)
2. seeking to explain and justify their research philosophy, methodologies, specific techniques and analytical approaches as well as deal with issues of reliability and validity
3. drawing out and stating the conclusions of their research. It is here that a comparison or reflective commentary on the relevant literature reviewed is commonly required and undertaken.

Clearly, the main focus of the first literature review should be your research topic or question(s). The focus of the second aspect is the literature on research philosophies and methodologies as they are employed in your research. The third focus of the research usually collects and collates aspects of both the first two literature reviews. In this third instance you not only relate what you have found to other literature and writings, but also identify (some would say admit) the strengths and limitations of your own research methodologies and any instruments (eg questionnaires) that you developed or utilized in your research.

> **TIP**
>
> When reviewing the literature on your chosen research topic it is advisable to use original sources. It is often preferable, however, when discussing research philosophies and methodologies as well as the construction of any instruments, to start with general compendium texts (eg Cohen and Manion, 1994) and move to the specialist methodology texts later. The appropriateness of particular methodologies for your research is not always immediately apparent, so general texts are good for providing overviews as well as advice on where to go for the more specialized literature.

GENERIC REVIEW CAPABILITIES

Within the thesaurus for 'review' the key words used were:

- exploration (the ability to probe the literature in terms of own research interests)
- analysis (the capability to dissect and scrutinize literature)
- discussion (the capability to identify and examine comparisons and contrasts)
- criticism (the capability to identify and explain strengths and deficiencies)
- summary (the capability to draw together different strands into a coherent whole).

These words and their associated activities are descriptors of what we call generic review capabilities – the attributes needed to be able to carry out a good literature review. While at times we may despair of ever being able to do this, all of the capabilities can be acquired, but to do so does require practice. Researchers need to be able accurately to describe and portray the writings of others, analyse those writings, evaluate the reasoning used as well as recognize the implications for their intended research of what is being said. What is unfortunate is that often many of these aspects, such as identifying underlying assumptions, the stages of an argument, and outcomes, are not made overt by authors, but have to be 'dug out' from the text.

ACTIVITY

Reviewing yourself, score yourself out of ten (with ten being perfect) in each of the generic review capabilities identified below. Does your score imply that you have some personal development to undertake? Where appropriate, develop an action plan to practise any review capability so as to enhance its effectiveness.

Exploration (probing the literature)   [   ]
Analysis (dissecting and scrutinizing literature)   [   ]
Discussion (examining comparisons and contrasts)   [   ]
Criticism (identifying and explaining strengths and deficiencies)   [   ]
Summary (drawing together the strands into a coherent whole)   [   ]

SCORE

ACTION PLAN FOR IMPROVEMENT

Practice does help us improve. We tend to develop these capabilities as we go through the education system on the basis of the increased practice that it provides. Researchers should never become complacent about generic review capabilities. They can always be improved, especially if they have not been used for some time. For those wanting to brush up on generic review capabilities, a good text to start with is Thomson (1996).

STARTING A LITERATURE REVIEW

Locating relevant literature

An important aspect of any research is the extent to which it is related to existing research and to theoretical perspectives produced by others. It is essential therefore that, fairly early on in the research process, a researcher locates and becomes familiar with the work conducted by other researchers and writers in their area of research.

The first job is to locate suitable locations of the literature, which usually means libraries. In many cases, the relevant libraries will be those associated with universities and colleges of further and/or higher education, large public libraries and those libraries linked to specialist agencies such as The British Council, teachers' centres, etc. It is very useful to visit such libraries and ascertain answers to the following questions.

- What is the range, number and quality of books in the area of interest?
- What is the range, number and quality of journals in the area of interest?
- Are all the books and journals that you may need reasonably accessible?
- What particular databases or abstracts of articles does the library hold – both paper based and on CD-ROM – that are useful for your research?
- Does the library have the capability to conduct on-line (Internet) literature searches, either specifically provided by a service agent or generally?
- Does the library have inter-library loan facilities and, if so, how long does it normally take to acquire loans and at what cost?
- What photocopying facilities are available to researchers?
- Is it possible to obtain microfiche copies, theses and dissertations from other libraries?
- What are the library's opening hours?
- Are qualified library staff available during these opening hours to assist if needed?

Check out what sorts of borrowing and reading rights to a library you can have, and what the costs are (if any). You may be able to get reading rights (where you have the right to use books and journals in a library but not borrow them) and/or borrowing rights (the right to take books out of the library to read). Libraries rarely, if ever, allow journals to be borrowed, though you can often photocopy articles for your own research purposes. Libraries can also facilitate access to other libraries, and provide letters of support enabling you to use other libraries.

It is possible, of course, to attempt to buy all the books and journals that you may want – but that is both expensive and wasteful. We do recommend, however, the purchase of the really significant texts central for the research so that they are handy for reference and dipping into as the research progresses.

Constructing a bibliography prior to reading

It is extremely useful early on in a research project to get together a list of books and articles that relate to the topic chosen for investigation. This is to give the researcher an idea of the breadth and nature of literature and research available in the area of interest. This list is the basis of the later bibliography. A bibliography is different from a set of references, for references are texts that are used directly and/or referred to in the research report. A bibliography contains all those references that have been reviewed in the process of carrying out and reporting on the research. It will usually include the work of the most respected researchers and writers in the chosen area.

There are basically two ways to construct a bibliography. The first, and less recommended way, is to construct a bibliography by serial reading – what some researchers call 'snowballing'. That is, you read a book or article (see active reading, p90) and then follow up on other books and articles either recommended or used by the author and usually contained in their bibliography or references. This approach is unlikely to provide you with a full grasp of the range of literature, however, for all authors are prisoners of their own literature review and research questions! Relying on other authors to provide you with a bibliography, therefore, can mean your missing important literature that either the other author(s) did not know about or did not like and hence did not refer to. While serial reading or snowballing can be useful, it is important to realize its limitations.

The second approach is to carry out a systematic search using library catalogues (eg *Books in Print*) and any available paper-based abstracts (eg journals such as *Technical Education Abstracts, Psychological Abstracts, Sociology of Education Abstracts*) or electronically stored data bases (eg CD-ROMs and the Internet). Many libraries have links via JANET and EARN (academic research networks) to national and international catalogues. Typically, libraries have compendia of key words that you can use to search for materials. While a competent researcher should be able to do these things themselves (see the activity below), any librarian should be able to assist in the development of a bibliography. Make sure that the literature obtained by any of these methods is directly relevant to the research topic and is up to date.

ACTIVITY

Identify a topic relevant to the research being carried out or contemplated. Obtain and use the relevant CD-ROM (eg international Educational Resources Information Center (USA) (ERIC) for education articles) and using the easy search mode (a process where you type in the key words, against which a complete search is carried out) carry out a bibliographic search of articles. For books, use another CD-ROM such as Books in Print, though the same research terms can be used. Typically, the results can either be looked through there and then, or be copied on to a floppy computer disk to be looked at later, or printed out for a hard (paper-based) copy that can be taken away.

> **TIP**
>
> When constructing bibliographies always work backwards in time from the current year to ensure 'up to dateness'. If lots of references are coming up it usually means that the research focus and terms are too broad and need narrowing down so as to ensure a proper focus and a realistically sized bibliography.

It may be that the number of articles or books in your research area is overwhelming. In this case it may well be necessary to reduce the field of operation by:

- reducing the time-scale of the search so that, for instance, the search covers the last five years rather than the last ten
- reducing the geographical area so that one might look at, say, just the United Kingdom rather than Europe as a whole, or the USA
- refining the focus of the research questions and making them more specific; for instance, in researching an aspect of the teaching of English a researcher may decide to restrict their study to secondary schools.

On the other hand it is quite possible that, if the topic is very live, new and up to date, there may be virtually no materials in the research literature which appear to be relevant. Other resources such as newspapers, weekly and/or monthly journals and magazines may then have to be used. Overall, however, while this may be true for specific topics, it is very rare for there to be no relevant literature. If one were looking at the implementation of a new technology or innovation into an organization, for example, then it is possible to find many references to the management of change, organizational theory and adult psychology, all of which may well be relevant to the study. 'Change' and 'innovation' are topics that have been with us for some time, so there is plenty of information and discussion in the literature about them. The researcher does, however, have to make the connections between what is read and their own research questions.

Example search approaches

There are a number of other approaches to developing a bibliography, such as consulting the many specialist reference sources. Existing theses and dissertations in the public domain are to be found in the *Index to*

Theses Accepted for Higher Degrees in the Universities of Great Britain and Ireland (Association of Special Libraries and Information Bureaux (Aslib), published quarterly) and the *British Education Theses Index* (Libraries and Schools of Education, 1983).

For the United States, the appropriate reference is *Dissertation Abstracts International* (University Microfilms International, USA), which is subdivided according to focus. Section A, for instance, is devoted to the Humanities and Social Sciences.

Many abstracting publications are also now available on paper and/or electronically. Examples include: *ANBAR Management Services Abstracts*, itself divided into four sections (Accounting, Marketing, Personnel and Training, and Top Management); *Applied Social Sciences Index and Abstracts*; and *Contents Pages in Education*.

The important thing to remember is to ask the librarians, who will be only too pleased to help.

There are also current bibliographies, such as the *British National Bibliography* (UK) and *Cumulative Book Index* (USA) and the *Social Sciences Citation Index*, which lists publications under the source of citations of those publications.

Then there are government publications, daily and weekly newspapers and the particular 'trade journals' such as the *Times Educational Supplement*. The various research councils also have their own publications and research listings.

All in all, there are a large number of sources of help. Getting hold of the literature may be more tricky, though an ex-tutor of ours always said that a person should 'beg, steal or borrow' – though not necessarily in that order! Reading rights, reservations, inter-library loans and buying books and articles are all potential sources. There is often a gap between ordering a reference and actually having it to read – so be patient. However you obtain your literature, ensure that you read as the research progresses, so that there is no backlog and so that the literature and reading can influence your views, research questions, methods of data collection and analysis. It is to that reading of materials that we now turn.

TIP

Always work backwards in time from the current day when carrying out a literature review. Obtain an overview first of what sources are available before deciding what to access and use.

IDENTIFYING AN AUTHOR'S AIMS

All written reports of research, whether dissertations or articles in research journals, contain a review of the previous work which is related to the topic under investigation. It is essential that you fully understand what others have done and found out, how they did it and what can be learned from it. This is so that you are able to compare your results with those of previous studies and so add to the pool of knowledge and understanding.

When reading books or articles, a device that we have found very useful is the mnemonic AIM. A mnemonic is a shorthand way of remembering something – in this case a way of reading. AIM is also an acronym, with each letter being the first letter of another word – Author's Intended Message.

Always approach any reading with regard to your research with your own question: 'What is the author trying to tell me or convince us of?' By taking such an approach, you become involved in *active reading*.

Active reading is the opposite of passive reading – the reading of words in a passage without thinking unduly about them. Active reading thus involves thinking about the words being used. In effect, the researcher continually asks: 'What do I think is meant by that word or sentence?' and/or 'On the basis of the words I have read, what would I expect the message or important points to be?'

Active reading is, in a way, entering into a conversation with the author by proxy or at a distance. As you cannot (usually) ask authors directly what they meant you have to converse or vigorously think about the meanings of their words in your own head.

An example of active reading

How do you carry out active reading? Here is a small example, based solely on the active reading of a title of a book.

ACTIVITY

Write down what you would expect to read were you to see a book entitled *Further and Higher Education Partnerships: The Future for Collaboration.*

We recently had the opportunity to read just such a book. Before we got so far as to open it we pondered the title, both what we thought it meant and what we would expect to find in such a book.

When we mulled over the title, *Further and Higher Education Partnerships: The Future for Collaboration*, we considered that it implied that further and higher education partnerships already exist – otherwise why their future? We considered that it also implied that the book was likely to contain examples or case studies of partnerships that are or have been successful – otherwise why suggest their expansion or further development? We further decided that the emphasis must be on collaboration, not competition, so the outcomes of such collaborations must be beneficial to both further and higher education – or else why have them? We thought also that the authors might be suggesting additional ways of developing existing patterns – otherwise why the future for collaboration? We considered that there might be some guidelines or sets of principles – presumably derived from experiences and current practices – that would be useful for systematizing existing relationships, developing them further, or even establishing new partnerships. We speculated also that there might be some tales of caution – things not to do – so the book might contain examples of stillborn or poor partnerships that resulted in conflict and anguish.

All these items were surmised from the title, based on an active reading principle of trying to identify at the outset what we would be likely to find in the book. We were not disappointed. The book was actually broken down into three sections: Framework for Partnership, Case Studies of Partnership, and The Future of Partnerships. Everything that we thought would be in the book was, as were some additional things that we later found beneficial to read.

What we have done in this exercise is suggest a modified version of the old adage that 'you should not judge a book by its cover' (or title) – though it will often give you a good idea of the contents! We have added that you can tell a great deal from it, especially if you engage in an active reading, questioning approach. Technically, active reading is the development of an advance organizer.

TIP

Do not be put off if your initial attempts at active reading do not seem to be working – it really is the case that practice makes perfect!

So far the AIM process has dealt with only the title, and what can be anticipated in reading an article or a book from its title. This approach does of course assume that titles are an accurate reflection of the contents!

The next steps in AIM

What is the next step? The answer to some extent lies with what is being read. If there is an abstract, then that should be the item read next. Again, assuming that the abstract is accurate – which is not always the case – active reading should inform you yet more clearly what the article or the book is about. Typically, good abstracts are a pithy answer to three questions:

1. what the topic is (and possibly why the topic is of interest to you)
2. the basic outlines of the research approach or approach to the topic
3. what the main finding(s) are.

We hope you will agree that, were these questions answered, the abstract should be able to confirm what you thought the article or the book was about that you had gained from an active reading of the title. Even if the abstract is not a particularly good one there ought to be sufficient there for you to add to the understanding that you are constructing without actually reading the complete work.

But what should you do next? One or both of two things: to develop your understanding still further, you should read any conclusion(s) and/or the bibliography, where these are available. The rationale for reading the conclusion(s) should be clear. If your understanding as a result of the title and abstract are accurate you should have this understanding confirmed by the conclusion(s). In addition to a reprise of different aspects of the abstract, the conclusions normally also state any shortcomings and/or implications for future research and development. This last item should add to your understanding also, so it is yet another step forward.

The rationale for an active perusal of the bibliography is straightforward too. We personally find reading bibliographies addictive, the reason being that authors invariably list or reference sources they have found useful, and/or those they have used to develop their own ideas, concepts and arguments. Reading bibliographies will help you fill in your understanding of what the article or book is about – but again it requires active reading to get the most out of it.

> **TIP**
>
> Authors tend to reference other books, articles and authors that agree with or support their own argument or thesis. Active reading of such bibliographies will give you further indications of the approach of the author(s) to the topic(s) that are their focus.

Typically, the next items you should read are any subheadings in the article. Alternatively you could read the introduction, though by now you may be getting blasé about what the article or book contains. It does not hurt to confirm or modify as appropriate your understanding of the article or book so far. Reading the subheadings, however, gives you an overview of how the book or article is constructed. You should use active reading again with each subheading to get some idea of what each section is likely to contain.

By now you should have a very good idea of what the article or book contains – what the theme or thesis is as well as some of the detail of its contents. At this stage you will have to decide whether or not to read the article or book in full, for you will know by this stage whether it is germane to your concerns. In research, remember, time is often in short supply, so you should read only those articles or books that are relevant to you or which, out of interest, you want to read. If it is the latter reason you should put it aside for holidays or other times when you are not so pushed for time.

MAKING NOTES

The process of making notes is a vital though very individual one. There are some useful guidelines that are worth remembering and practising that will help to cut down the amount of time you spend making notes. Start by working out a system for recording your notes. This can best be done using either a computer or a set of index cards. The principles are the same, but notes put straight on to a computer are immediately available for writing up and/or inserting as quotes and references.

Using a computer from the outset can save you a lot of time and problems of presentation. With the progressive emphasis on the curriculum at all ages being concerned with the development and application of key skills (eg Hodkinson *et al.*, 1996) you can increasingly expect to be required to provide your research report or thesis word processed. Furthermore, the requirements for word processed presentation often involve the use of visual aids for presentation of data such as pie charts and histograms. Putting notes on to a computer also short-circuits your having to type them in from cards when you are constructing your report, research article or thesis.

If you do not use a computer to keep track of references, index cards are an immense help, as you can shuffle them so that you always have the correct alphabetical and date order.

If what you present is a summary of the position, viewpoint or research findings of an author in general, then it is often acceptable just to provide the author and date (the Harvard system, see p97), though we would *strongly recommend* that you include the page number also. This page referencing can be very useful if someone (as, for instance, in a viva voce) contests your understanding of what an author has written. Page numbering demonstrates your confidence in your understanding of the literature.

TIP

When typing up quotes, make sure that you provide the full bibliographic reference in your notes for use when using the quote and providing the reference. This should *always* include the page numbers.

Page numbering also makes sure that you are not guilty (knowingly or unknowingly) of plagiarism. Plagiarism is the process of passing someone else's work off as your own. In most situations where plagiarism occurs and is found out there are severe penalties. Where your research is part of a course or programme of study it is not uncommon to find plagiarism losing credits, and perhaps even leading to your being required to leave the course or programme. In our opinion nothing is worth that.

COMPARING AND CONTRASTING AUTHORS

There will usually be more than one perspective on the topic(s) you are researching. It thus becomes very important to be able to compare and contrast authors. If you have carried out active reading with each piece of literature you should have a good idea of what it contains. If you then make notes you should be careful to identify the different stages of their arguments. That way, you can compare and contrast the authors, based on the following.

- Which authors (more or less) say the same, and which say different things?
- What do they say differently? Do their assertions start from the same, similar or different assumptions?
- Do their arguments or propositions follow logically and rationally from each other?
- Are their arguments or logic rational and acceptable (and if so, why)?
- What does each author say about the others?
- What is the relevance or impact of their points of view on your research topic(s) and concern(s)?

A good way of bringing out similarities and differences is to identify actual quotations that reflect the essence or the arguments of each author. Doing this gives you ready materials for inclusion in your research report or dissertation.

Again, putting quotes straight on to a computer is the best way, for it is then a matter of 'cutting and pasting' into your report, dissertation or thesis. If you cannot access a computer a set of index cards with the quotes written on them is a good alternative, for then you can shuffle the cards to arrive at an order of use when you want to write individual chapters or sections.

TIP

When identifying quotes use either their direct relevance to your research or the extent to which the quotes clearly show up the different positions of the separate authors as your standard of measurement for inclusion or omission.

WRITING UP YOUR LITERATURE REVIEW

Once you have finished collecting and reviewing the literature you have then only to write it up! Unfortunately there are no easy ways to accomplish this. It is useful, however, to plan the review out beforehand in note form so that the right order and flow of argument, proposition and debate is achieved. Remember, though, that ultimately, *what is written should be germane to the research focus and concerns*.

A literature review is not just a question of displaying knowledge and erudition. Rather, it is evaluated by the extent to which the survey illuminates and carries forward the research interests and concerns. The literature review should not include literature for its own sake.

TIP

When the literature survey has been written check the following.

- Has the emphasis been on the most important and relevant authors and works?
- Are the sources up to date?
- Is the survey critical of authors and their work where appropriate?
- Does the literature review focus on the research concerns and questions (and not deviate)?
- Does it read well?

If at all possible, ask some other people to read the literature review, for in writing authors can often get too close to their work and miss items or connections.

USING QUOTATIONS IN THE TEXT

Typically, research projects and dissertations are typed or word processed using double-line spacing for the text. Quotations are usually provided using single-line spacing, though quotations which are longer than one line should also be indented. It is relatively unusual to include quotes of longer than seven lines, though if it sustains your argument it is acceptable. At the end of the quote you should include the author's surname, year of publication and the page number of the quotation.

Referring to others in the text

In the Harvard system (which we favour, though there are other systems available) at every point in the text at which reference is made to other writers the name of the writer and the year of publication should be included. If the surname of the author is part of the sentence, then the year of the publication will appear in brackets, eg:

Smith (1993) describes this . . .

If the name of the author is not part of the sentence then both the surname and the year of publication are in brackets, eg:

In a recent study (Smith, 1990) it is described as . . .

If there are two authors then both family names should be given; if there are three or more authors the first author's family name should be given, followed by *et al.*, eg:

Smith and Jones (1993) suggest that . . .

In a recent study (Smith and Jones, 1993) it is suggested . . .

The most recent work (Smith *et al.*, 1993) shows that . . .

If the same author has published two or more works in the same year then each work should be referred to individually by the year followed by lower case letters (a, b, c, etc). (These different references should be included in the bibliography.) For example:

Smith (1993a) shows how . . .

When you need to refer to two or more different parts of a work or are quoting directly you should include the page numbers after the year of publication.

Smith (1993, p112) gives a model to explain . . .

THE PRESENTATION OF THE BIBLIOGRAPHY

Citing books

The bibliography comes at the end of your project report or dissertation. The citations are listed as either bibliography or references, which are then arranged alphabetically by authors' names and then, where necessary, by date and letter. Single-author books and articles appear before co-authored articles and books by the same author, with the earliest dated first. Where there is more than one reference for an author in any one year, the order is alphabetical by title, and lower case letters added to denote more than one publication in that year.

The citations should follow a standard format, such as Harvard, unless another format is specified. If another format is not specified, the use of either underlining or italics is acceptable, though the style should be consistent throughout. The presentation should be: Author's family name, comma, initials of first name(s), year of publication in brackets, title of the book in upper and lower case underlined or in italics, comma, edition (if applicable followed by comma), publisher, comma, place of publication, full stop. There are examples below.

Books and articles often have more than one author. The names of all the authors should be given in the bibliography in the order presented by the authors themselves, linked by the word 'and' for the last named. Again there are examples below.

Atkinson, R L, Atkinson, R C and Hilgard, E R (1983) *Introduction to Psychology*, 5th ed, Harcourt Brace Jovanovich, New York.

Blyth, W A L and Derricot, R (1977) *The Social Significance of Middle Schools*, Batsford, London.

Crystal, D (1971) *Linguistics*, Penguin, Harmondsworth.

Trudgill, P (1974a) *The Social Differentiation of English in Norwich*, Cambridge University Press.

Trudgill, P (1974b) *Sociolinguistics: An introduction*, Penguin, Harmondsworth.

Trudgill, P (1978) *Sociolinguistics Patterns in British English*, Edward Arnold, London.

Citing articles in journals

A slightly different format is used when citing contributions to journals: author's family name, comma, initials of first name(s), comma, year of publication in brackets, title of contribution in upper and lower case and in quotation marks, comma, title of the periodical or journal underlined or in italics, comma, volume number in bold (heavy) type, issue number, comma, the page numbers of the article prefaced by pp, full stop. An example is:

Best, D (1985) 'Primary and secondary qualities: waiting for an educational Godot', *Oxford Review of Education*, **1** 1, pp73–84.

Citing contributions in books

Where books are made up of contributions from a variety of authors the following order and format should be used. Cite author's surname, comma, initials of first name(s), comma, year of publication in brackets, then the title of the contribution in upper and lower case and in quotation marks, comma, followed by 'in', the editor's surname followed by a comma, the initials then (ed), the title of the book in upper and lower case underlined or in italics, comma, publisher, comma, place of publication, comma, page numbers, full-stop. For example:

Labov, W (1968) 'The reflection of social processes in linguistic structures', in Fishman, J A (ed) *Readings in the Sociology of Language*, Mouton, The Hague, pp47–63.

Government publications

These should be cited as follows: name of the responsible department, year of publication in brackets, title of the publication in upper and lower case underlined or in italics, comma, publisher, comma, place of publication. If there are official series codes these should be cited after the title, and if there is a chairperson then this name should be included at the end. For example:

Department of Education and Science (1985) *Education for All: Report of the committee of inquiry into the education of children from ethnic minority groups*, Cmnd 9453, HMSO, London (Swann Report).

Theses

Occasionally you may wish to quote from a thesis, and should follow this format: author's surname, comma, initial(s), year of award in brackets, title in upper and lower case underlined or in italics, comma, degree awarded followed by Thesis, comma and the name of the awarding institution. An example is:

Selmes, I P (1985) *Approaches to Learning at Secondary School: Their identification and facilitation*, PhD Thesis, University of Edinburgh.

Mimeographed materials

Mimeographs refer to duplicated materials, such as papers presented to conferences but not formally published. The information required is: name of the author(s) and initials, the date, the title of the paper, the circumstances under which the paper was presented, and the fact that it was mimeoed (duplicated). The title of the paper is in quotation marks and has initial capitals. For example:

Adams, R G (1968), 'Aspects of Documentation in the Social Sciences', paper presented to the 1968 Annual Conference of the British Educational Management and Administration Society, mimeo.

SUMMARY

The stages in the literature search process are as follows:

1. What is/are the research questions that have been focused upon?
2. What key words were included for search purposes?
3. What related research key words are deliberately excluded?
4. What is the most appropriate bibliographic search procedure?
5. Which books?
6. Which abstracting journals?
7. Which journals?
8. Which search terms should be used on a CD-ROM?
9. Are there sufficient materials or is it necessary to widen the area of inquiry?
10. Are there any relevant theses and/or dissertations?
11. Has it been possible to clearly identify each author's AIM?
12. Has the 'important' rather than 'less important' (even if interesting) information been dealt with?
13. Does the review synthesize the selected literature into a coherent whole that clearly relates to the research focus and questions?
14. Does the presentation:
    - cohere?
    - develop a theme or themes?
    - clearly relate to the problem to be researched?
    - demonstrate a critical stance towards existing literature where appropriate?

This final point is very important, since many myths have been perpetrated by readers not being sufficiently critical of other researchers' techniques and conclusions.

TIP

Do look in theses, dissertations and research articles for their bibliographic reviews, usually to be found near the beginning. Even if the survey is not in your area of interest, you should get some ideas on how to construct and write a literature survey.

LOOKING AHEAD: WRITING UP THE CONCLUSION

When writing up a research project, link what has been found or the conclusions developed to the original literature review. If certain themes in the literature became apparent as worthy of investigation, to what extent have those themes been developed, modified, changed or proven by the research?

Be cautious when making bold statements. A touch of humility is always beneficial, as is an awareness of the necessity for further research, either to replicate (or not) the research findings or to address related issues and concerns. A reflection on the whole process is also useful, if only to ensure that you do not forget the lessons that have been learned during the process of writing up your literature review.

7

Research and Organizations

INTRODUCTION AND OVERVIEW

It has become commonplace in recent years for researchers to wish to undertake a study of a particular organization. For many researchers, however, this is often not just any organization, but the one in which they work. While there may be ethical, validity and reliability problems with this, the intent is understandable. If one reflects further, however, such an intent suggests that organizations can be difficult places to understand; that is, it is not always clear what is going on! In most if not all organizational research, therefore, the researcher must work on the assumption that organizations are not all they seem. Indeed, were organizations so transparent, it could be argued that there would be no need to research them.

Moreover, organizations are becoming more and more complex. This is not a new phenomenon, nor is research into them, as evidenced by the classic studies and work on such diverse topics as bureaucracies (Weber, 1947) the comparative study of organizations (Etzioni, 1964), and commentaries going back to sixteenth-century Florence (Machiavelli, 1958). What this means is that the researcher must recognize and deal with that complexity, possibly by honing research questions that focus on aspects of the work and operations of an organization.

As this chapter deals with research in and on organizations – a subject so significant as to be worthy of entire books (eg Gordon, 1993; Dawson, 1992; Cassell and Symon, 1994 and Tsoukas, 1994), we will be selective and cover the topic from the point of new of the researcher's needs by using a number of subheadings. To do this, an initial definition of an organization is provided and reviewed, before we go on to consider researching at the organizational level, and then research within organizations. A number of issues and concerns will be raised that any researcher has to consider before and while doing research. In line with the interactive approach we have adopted, exercises and tips are included that will help you in carrying out research into organizations.

A DEFINITION OF AN ORGANIZATION

As we are concerned in this chapter with building up a picture of organizations, and of research of and in them, we will start with a relatively simple definition of an organization (Bennett, 1992):

Organizations are social entities deliberately created to achieve certain objectives. (p145)

This is an interesting definition, and worthy of some consideration. In order to assist you in that, the following exercise should prove useful. It is not easy, particularly the second part, so it may be helpful to respond to it on the basis of an organization that you know.

ACTIVITY

Rewrite, in your own words, the essence of an organization as defined by Bennett above. Following that, what are the key characteristics of organizations?

Aspect one: Organizations involve people and groups

It is clear from Bennett's definition that organizations must have at least two people in them. This is what is meant by the term 'social entity' (the word social means communal, common, collective). While it is possible legally for organizations to consist of individual people (thus making the researching of an organization the study of their behaviour within any given social context, such as a market-place), the study of organizations accepts that they normally comprise two or more people. Where those individuals are located together, and perform similar tasks, there is a strong impetus for social groups to form (a group being a number of people who share common norms of behaviour, perspectives and values).

A consequence for researchers of this assumption is that it becomes necessary to understand their view of the world, and the definitions of situations held by those different people who make up the organization. Additionally, there is often a comparing and contrasting of norms, perspectives and values between the different individuals and groups that make up the organization. This is because the study of people, and of people in organizations, requires not only or just the identification and recording of how they act and think. Research also requires an explanation, from the point of view of the participants, of why they do what they do or think what they think.

Research in and of organizations, therefore, requires the researcher to identify and examine the different perceptions and understandings that individuals and groups have of situations, their place within them, and what this means for the way they behave and what they do. This is very much an exercise in discursive practice, which Schwandt (1997) defines as:

> [the] particular ways of talking and writing about and doing or performing one's practice that are coupled with particular social settings in which those ways of talking are regarded as understandable and more or less valuable. (p31)

As Schwandt reminds us, such an approach makes it clear that language form, structure and use is both a key element of research in organizations and in the conceptual frameworks that are constructed. This hermeneutic emphasis is a key element in *verstehen* or understanding the social construction of the world as and by actors in ongoing situations.

Aspect two: Organizations are deliberately created

This aspect implies that organizations come about as a result of the intentions of key individuals, and are therefore planned deliberately and brought into existence. In many cases, of course, this is true. The history of almost all economic organizations and specific firms attest to the original intent, perspicacity and energy of the founders. What is important to remember, however, is that organizations can outlast their original founders, and thus possibly outlast the goals and intentions for which they were originally created.

As a result, researchers have to be careful of assuming that the intentions of the original founders were both known and clear cut (do we always know why we do things?) and remain substantially unchanged thereafter. If anything, because personnel change, and bring with them their own perceptions and values, it is highly unlikely that the original intentions remain in their original form, or still pertain.

A more significant problem, though, are those organizations that appear to come into existence without any overt deliberations by the participants. In the United Kingdom, for instance, queues form without any deliberate organizational impetus by any one individual. The definition, therefore, has problems with recognizing the power and significance of informal organizational structures that come into being. Groups may form that are social in the sense of people getting together, but that are not social in the sense that the activity may be personal and self-pleasing, with the involvement of other people being incidental. Possible examples here may be religious services and sports events.

For the researcher, therefore, this aspect of the definition makes it imperative that the deliberate creation of organizations, and of groups and groupings within organizations, be treated as a question to be asked and answered, not just accepted. Groups may be deliberately formed, or not, and it certainly cannot be assumed that the continued existence of the organization or groups within organizations is due to the conscious and deliberate intentions of all concerned. It may be, but equally it may not. This suggests that, while observation might be a suitable approach to the study of organizations, particularly in its participant observation format, it is in all probability insufficient to provide an account and understanding of the nature and significance of events, groups and organizations.

Aspect three: Organizations are dedicated to the pursuance of certain objectives

The origin of many organizations is clearly directly related to the founders' intention to achieve a number of goals. It has not always been the case, however, that those goals have been specified, shared or sustained through the years that an organization has been in existence. This is why, since the early 1980s, there has been an upsurge of interest in the creation and use of 'mission' and 'vision' statements by organizations (or, more correctly, by the top managers and personnel of organizations) (Peeke, 1995). Were the goals non-controversial, or easy to see and articulate, and accepted by all, there would be no need for such mission and vision statements.

What makes the situation and subsequent investigations more interesting for researchers, therefore, is that it is highly likely that not all goals are always formally expressed, perceived or seen by the whole staff of an organization. This can make researching organizations difficult, but it also means that research results have a tendency to be provisional: this is our research and understanding of this organization (or part of an organization if it is complex) at a particular moment in time.

The implications of the goal-oriented nature of organizations for researchers are several. While it is legitimate to research the goals of an organization (what they are, who holds them, how far they are spread through or down an organization, what degree of awareness and commitment there is by the different groups and individuals within the organization), one has to be careful of accepting management definitions of the goals as being the goals of the organization, or the only goals of the organization. Other groups may have different goals, such as 'having a quiet life'. These other goals may conflict directly with management goals, or at least interfere with the achievement of those goals, for as Parkin (1971) pointed out, there can be found in many organizations dominant, subordinate and contra-(oppositional) cultures. The articulation and researching of such differences or variations (where they exist) is a key task for researchers.

CHARACTERISTICS OF ORGANIZATIONS

The exercise above asked for a definition of the key characteristics of organizations. While there may be some variations on this if any particular organization was taken as the blueprint for a focus of analysis, most organizations exhibit all or most of the following characteristics:

- a set (and/or subsets) of (more or less) articulated goals and objectives to be achieved, and against which performance is measured
- a division of labour
- power and authority structures and decision-making processes
- a culture or cultures.

This list is very close to the different analytical perspectives that Bolman and Deal (1984) suggest can be used to research and analyse organizations. The word perspective is used to emphasize the way that the approach concentrates on certain aspects of the organization, and leaves other aspects in the dark or background. For Bolman and Deal a complete research programme and analysis of an organization would require all four perspectives, undoubtedly a difficult task to carry out on all but the smallest and simplest of organizations.

TIP

When studying organizations, try to identify as early as possible the parameters of your research in terms of focus and location. While it may be possible over a number of years to study a single site (say a school of 300 students and 12 teachers), the feasibility of studying holistically (all aspects of) a large organization of several thousand personnel on a number of sites, perhaps spread across several countries, is almost impossible.

PERSPECTIVES WITHIN ORGANIZATIONAL RESEARCH AND ANALYSIS

The perspectives that Bolman and Deal (1984) identify as appropriate to the study of organizations are:

- structural
- political
- cultural
- human resource.

Perspective one: Structural

The structural perspective focuses on the differentiation and specialization of tasks and jobs within the organization, and the associated development of specialist personnel to carry out those tasks and jobs. It is usually portrayed by an organizational chart, though that gives little information about how things get done. Different organizations do have different organizational structures, however, and the researching and analysis of these are central topics for those interested in organizational analysis.

One must be very careful of assuming that organizations are either monolithic (experienced or accepted exactly the same throughout the organization) or remain essentially unaltered during their period of existence. One model of organizational development, for instance, sees organizations as passing from a pioneer stage through a mature stage to a long-established, potentially ossifying stage (unless there is renewal) (Bennis *et al.*, 1994). Researching the state and needs of an organization is a key research task, well worthy of a research project.

The same can be said of that level of management thinking and decision making that is often seen as the preserve of senior management – strategic management. Here, current quality initiatives suggest that the emphasis should not only be on long-term planning but also on the creation and dissemination of mission and vision statements for the purposes of generating employee commitment to the organization (Peeke, 1995). Once the researcher starts to look closely at these aspects, however, they begin to slide over into other perspectives on organizations, including those of decision making or power.

ACTIVITY

Reflect on the structural perspective, and its emphasis in organizational charts that show lines of communication (formal and informal), spans of control, levels of decision making (eg strategic management) and accountability, and try to identify what research methods (eg documents of committees, organizational charts and flow charting, etc) you might use to research this perspective within any organization.

Perspective two: Political

The political perspective focuses on the distribution and use of power, authority and decision-making processes. Power is the ability to affect and/or control the behaviour and life chances of others, possibly even without their consent. Authority is an extension of this, as it is defined as power that is considered legitimate and accepted by those on whom it is focused. Decision-making processes are concerned with deciding who does what, when, where and how.

As the sources of power are various (eg charisma, control of information, possession of expertise, rules and tradition), can be both formal and informal (not based within the customary or prescribed structures and decision-making processes), and be contestable, researchers have a major part to play in analysing the distribution and use of power.

ACTIVITY

Reflect on the political perspective, and its emphasis on the deployment and experience of power, particularly in decision-making processes, and try to identify what research methods (eg interviews, stakeholder analysis, etc) you might use to research the perspective within any organization.

Some theorists (eg Clegg 1989) go further, and see power as *the* key concept in researching organizations, with the range of perspectives available within that overall approach being legion. Lukes (1974), for instance, has a radical perspective upon power as being able to set the parameters of action and decision making, thereby managing what questions organizational members are allowed to ask or contest. An even more radical approach is that of Foucault (1977), whose micro-politics of power concentrate on the surveillance and disciplinary nature of power within organizations. It is indeed powerful stuff!

Perspective three: Cultural

The cultural perspective for the researching and analysis of organizations focuses on the sets of ideas, attitudes, values and norms of behaviour that govern and/or affect the individuals and groups who espouse or belong to them. At one level, because all the members of an organization are part of it, there has to be a minimal level of acceptance of a corporate culture for the organization to continue. But so as not to get carried away with this assumption of commonality and all pervasiveness generating high levels of commitment, it is useful to remember that prisons are organizations, or more precisely total organizations (Goffman, 1961). We would not say necessarily that prisoners are committed to the organization in the cultural sense as well as in the physical sense.

The implications of this perspective for research on organizations are enormous. For a start, the cultural perspective sensitizes the researcher to cultural differences between individuals and groups, often manifested through territorial claims and adornment, including the unique, the unusual, the odd, the peculiar, the special and the extra-ordinary aspects of organizational values, beliefs, ideas and behaviour. Such multifarious, sundry and varied cultural aspects are worthy of research, as are differences that are systematically related to both internal and external factors, such as level and type of job, family and socio-economic background, ethnicity, gender and religion.

Second, the perspective raises issues about what the culture(s) of any organization actually are. Rather, the perspective makes it important to identify the different cultures or the range of cultures that exist within organizations – particularly large organizations with significant divisions of labour. We have noted already the work of Parkin (1971) on dominant cultures, subordinate cultures (sub-cultures that are different but articulated within the overall dominant cultural framework) and contra-cultures (cultures that deliberately oppose the dominant culture to varying degrees of overtness), which we believe essential to any research on cultures, but other writers are significant also (eg Wuthnow, 1984).

As culture can be defined as either a system of knowledge or concepts and/or a system of material artefacts, technologies and physical settings or constraints (buildings, etc), so research into culture can either take an approach that concentrates on identifying, describing and analysing the perspectives of individuals or groups, or identifying, describing and analysing the impact of the material environment on the activities and ways of thinking of individuals and groups.

These two ways have often been conceptualized as the ideational and materialist perspectives, and lead to different research foci. Hargreaves (1978), for instance, using a basically materialist perspective, articulates and applies to teachers' activities within organizations the concept of 'coping strategies' – ways in which individuals and groups make out or muddle through situations and events in the face of external constraints and requirements. Alternatively, Czarniawska and Sevon (1996) locate their analysis and associated research on 'translating organizational change' firmly in the realm of ideas and perceptions. Both are right, and neither is wrong – they are just different ways of researching and analysing organizations. The choice depends on the research interests and underlying theoretical frameworks of the researcher.

ACTIVITY

Reflect on the cultural perspective, and its emphasis on the articulation and embodiment of ideas, values and beliefs in behaviour and material artefacts that subsequently constrain our behaviour; try to identify what research methods (eg interviews, discourse analysis, etc) you might use to research the perspective within any organization.

Perspective four: Human resource

The human resource (HR) perspective focuses on the development and capability of people and groups within an organization as well as the extent to which it dovetails organizational needs and desires with the desires of individual staff members and groups of staff so as to maximize their contributions and production or service outcomes.

The HR approach to organizational research takes as its starting point organizational goals. Popularized in the 1980s by Peters and colleagues (eg 1982, 1987) it is based on the assumption that an organization has goals and, in pursuing those goals, can become even more effective than it currently is (Guest, 1990). This approach, which has close ties to the quality movement (Wilkinson and Wilmott, 1995), but which also has links to increased efforts by managers to control all that takes place within an organization (Pollitt, 1993), has become a major focus of organizational research in the 1990s.

The eight management principles of Peters and Waterman (1982) were seen as being HR based. They were identified as follows:

1. a bias for action ('do it, fix it, try it')
2. closeness to the customer – a commitment to listening to their wants
3. encouragement of autonomy and entrepreneurship within the organization
4. respect for the rank and file employee/resistance to 'we/they' attitudes to management/other work relations
5. emphasis on a few core organizational values (eg reliability, attention to detail)
6. concentration on activities the organization knows and understands ('stick to the knitting')
7. simple organizational structures with lean top-level staff
8. a combination of centralization of core values/philosophy with maximum decentralization of operations.

These principles – derived from a study of the best-performing organizations in the USA, are a mix of a number of perspectives and activities, including strategic planning and focus, decision making, organizational structures and operations, and the utility of a cultural core for the organization. For the HR perspective, however, the emphasis particularly is upon gain through employees – which means the necessity to look after all the core human resource aspects of an organization, such as:

- organizational charts, job designs, descriptions and key effectiveness areas
- recruitment and selection
- induction and management of new employees
- training and development
- organizational culture and climate
- leadership
- health and safety
- pay scales and conditions of service

- career planning, including progression and substitution
- appraisal and review.

These are significant topics, well worth researching, either individually or comparatively across organizations.

ACTIVITY

Reflect on the human resource perspective, and its emphasis on the aspects listed above. Pick an area that appeals to you and try to identify what research methods (eg questionnaires, focus groups, etc) you might use to research the perspective within any organization.

POSSIBLE TOPICS IN ORGANIZATIONAL RESEARCH

This section is included as a sort of summary, for only with the utmost difficulty, and requiring space far beyond this chapter, could we display the topics that have been and/or are capable of being researched in relation to organizations. We have provided suggestions for a number of areas throughout the chapter drawn from a range of sources. Because of this an example of the focus of organizational research and analysis taken from the literature will be used now to show at least some further possible areas for research.

A suitable schema is provided by Judith Gordon's *A Diagnostic Approach to Organizational Behaviour* (1993). In explaining her title, Gordon prefers to use the word 'diagnosis' as a shorthand way of 'describing, understanding, explaining and predicting behaviour in organizations'. Gordon divides the book into areas dealing with individual and group issues, organizational design and development, as shown in Figure 7.1. She provides case studies, exercises and research possibilities throughout the book, making it a good source of ideas and materials for use in a research process.

No one approach is better than any other. Gordon suggests that this is because:

the understanding of any organizational situation includes the ability to analyse it in a number of ways, rather than to assume that any one explanation is adequate. (Preface)

This is a position we certainly agree with.

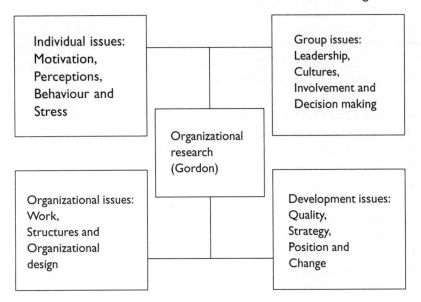

Figure 7.1 *A schematic view of topics in organizational research (after Gordon, 1993)*

POSSIBLE RESEARCH METHODS

This chapter has already suggested that there are a range of research methods both suitable and available for organizational researchers. While it is acceptable to study organizations for their own sake, some researchers do not consider this enough. These are action researchers and action learners who, by using interventions and studying the effects of those interventions, attempt to improve the organization and the lot of the staff within it (eg McGill and Beaty, 1992 and Zuber-Skerrett, 1996). Cassell and Symons (1994) concur with this active approach, for they write,

> Organizational research is fundamentally a practical endeavour. Researchers address the very real problems that organizations are facing in the 1990s and often require a wide range of techniques depending upon the demands of the clients with whom they have to deal. (p9)

How the research is actually carried out is an open question. As the title of their book suggests, Cassell and Symons (1994) see qualitative methods as perhaps more appropriate to the study of organizations than quantitative methods, though the latter do have a place. Moreover, they are concerned to acquaint readers with the diverse range of methods available, such as:

- qualitative research interviews
- the 20 statements test
- verbal protocol techniques
- repertory grid techniques
- discourse analysis
- participant observation
- group methods
- content analysis
- tracer studies
- stakeholder analysis
- case studies
- intervention techniques.

This is indeed a wide range of techniques and methods. But if the intention is to research organizations we have no alternative but to be creative in how we conduct that research. To be authentic and true to the realities of organizational life and concerns is a task worthy of any researcher.

8

Quality Improvement and Research in Organizations

INTRODUCTION AND OVERVIEW

The previous chapter identified some of the different ways of studying organizations *as* organizations. In addition to this approach, however, there are many forms of research related to quality improvement, evaluation research and action research that are carried out within organizations by managers and other staff. Such activities are under-taken for the purposes of controlling and managing business affairs, including development activities, more effectively. This chapter focuses on such research aspects.

It is often the case that those members of staff who feel some responsibility to try and improve their practice do not actually see themselves as researchers. This is perhaps understandable where people define research as being heavily statistical, quantitative, or involving experimentation with control groups, etc. This does not alter the fact that research is what managers and other individuals or groups are doing. While there may be questions about the degrees of formality, systematism or thoroughness of what they do, in research terms, those are questions of validity and reliability, not about whether or not it is research.

Given this concern with the improvement of the quality of practice, this chapter initially provides a brief definition of quality and the key components of a quality approach. There follows a brief section on the management cycle of activity, and the role of monitoring and evaluation within that cycle, before we move on to identify and discuss the various types of evaluation. Finally, we concentrate on audits as a form of monitoring *and* evaluation.

A DEFINITION OF QUALITY AND ITS COMPONENTS

As this is a book on research it is not the place to go in detail into the debates over quality, for that is best covered elsewhere (eg Doherty, 1994). However, we do still need to have an acceptable definition of quality.

ACTIVITY

Reflect upon your reading and/or experience of quality in organizations. Write a sentence or two on how you believe quality is or can be defined.

For a variety of reasons (eg whether or not you have studied or had practical experience) you may have found the activity to be easy or hard. Whichever, it is important to recognize that definitions of quality are related to intentions ('Our mission is to provide the best possible service or manufactured article in the sector'). Additionally, there are a number of different approaches to quality, and a range of different quality awards (eg the Baldridge Award, the Deming Prize, ISO 9000), which all take slightly different approaches. A familiar feature of all such definitions and quality awards is their emphasis on 'fitness for purpose', with the purpose being defined by those people who buy the goods or services being offered; that is, the good or service should meet and/or satisfy the needs of those people who purchase it.

One common form of quality application in organizations is total quality management (TQM). Dale and Plunkett (1995) view TQM thus:

a management philosophy embracing all activities through which the needs and expectations of the customer and the community, and the objectives of the organization are satisfied in the most efficient and cost-effective way by maximizing the potential of all employees in a continuing drive for improvement. (p2)

Key words and concepts are philosophy, customers, efficiency, effectiveness, employee involvement and continuous improvement. One author has now gone so far as to suggest that in TQM employees now have two jobs – the one they are employed to do and the job of doing it better (Evans, 1995). While there may be a certain amount of hyperbole in this, the emphases of Dale and Plunkett are mirrored in much if not all of the quality literature and awards. Once an organization has embarked on a journey to quality there are no quick fixes, and no easy ways (Simmerman, 1994).

Kanji and Asher (1996) are even more precise about TQM. They suggest that the four principles of TQM are:

1. delight the customer
2. management by fact
3. people-based management
4. continuous improvement.

In turn, those four principles are associated with eight core concepts, as shown in Table 8.1.

Table 8.1 *Kanji and Asher's (1996) four principles and eight core concepts of TQM*

Principles	Core concepts
Delight the customer	Customer needs are identified and satisfied
	Customers are internal as well as external to the organization
Management by fact	All work consists of linked processes
	Measurement is essential
People-based management	Teamwork and involvement
	People make quality
Continuous improvement	Continuous improvement cycle
	Prevention of defect is better than repair

This is an impressive list. Without labouring the point, the core concepts clearly point to the necessity for systematic and routine data collection and analysis (what we call research), with an emphasis on change, development and improvement being particularly based on 'measurement' and 'facts'.

RESEARCH AND IDENTIFYING AND ASSESSING CUSTOMER NEEDS

From the references above it can be seen that, initially, there is a need for research on customer needs, and then into the design and delivery of goods and services to promote or achieve the subsequent satisfaction of those needs. Additionally, research activities of a monitoring, evaluation and improvement kind during the processes of production and delivery of a good or service are needed. These types of research are necessary to ensure that the quality of what is provided at least meets the customer's needs and, if possible, actually exceeds them. That is what is meant by delighting the customer!

Dale and Plunkett (1995) use the term 'customer' to refer to the purchasers of goods and services; to that concept of customer we add the concept of 'client'. While there is often seen to be an interchange between the two, we are clear that a client is the person who buys or pays for a good or service, while a customer is the person who actually uses or receives the good or service. The distinction is easy to remember by way of an example – a parent who buys a toy for their child is the client, the child is the customer!

A customer needs analysis, therefore, concentrates on identifying what the customers and/or clients want from a good or service. There are times, however, where for any number of reasons – age, illness, etc – the customer may not be able to tell us what they want. In situations such as these we refer to other stakeholders to the relationship (such as parents in the case of children), who have a stake in what is provided and something to offer the researcher about the desirable features of a good or service. A stakeholder can be defined as a person or group with a vested interest in a situation, including the provision of goods and services to themselves and others. The issue with multiple stakeholders, however, is problematic to a researcher, in that stakeholders can 'have different criteria for judging' (Flynn, 1996, p215).

Given any range of stakeholders, a full needs analysis will require the researcher to implement a stratified sample approach to data collection. As Fitz-Gibbon and Morris (1987) note:

> Stratifying requires that you select separately from among groups of people who differ according to some critical characteristic(s) which might affect their results. (p162)

ACTIVITY

Choose a service or a good with which you are familiar (eg a hospital or a car), and identify as many stakeholders as possible who might have an interest in ensuring that the service or good is 'fit for purpose' (delivers what is needed).

By identifying stakeholders you are effectively identifying the different constituencies that would make up the total sample in research. It should be obvious to you by now that any proportional sample which is less than 100 per cent should ensure that the sample of stakeholder sub-categories should be representative of the target population as a whole.

There may still be problems, however, for the concept of need is itself problematic. In identifying needs which a good or service is designed to meet, a need can be:

- *real* – an actual need a person has or category of people have
- *felt* – a need that a person or group feels they have that may or may not be real
- *expressed* – a need that is communicated, but that may not either be a felt or a real need
- *imputed* – a need that is expressed either because of comparison with others ('others have one and I want one') or because a third party (eg management) believes the need to be so.

As we are not always aware of our real needs the identification of needs can be very confusing, and even more difficult to research. Nonetheless some form of needs identification has to be carried out, particularly with the target group(s), as it is likely to engender an acceptance of the findings subsequently.

What is important is to uncover as much research data as possible. It is useful to conceive of the research process as being one concerned to uncover and analyse different levels of data (see Figure 8.1).

The first set of data is already in the public domain, and requires collation and analysis in the light of the needs of the researcher. The second level is that data on social life, activity, perspectives and understanding that can be obtained through primary research, for it is not yet collected, and even less subject to scrutiny and analysis. The third layer consists of the sort of data that is so tied up with our self-concepts and underlying cultural assumptions that we are either not aware of them, or can only articulate them with the greatest difficulty. At a personal level, that often is the field of psychoanalysis.

Customer, client and stakeholder needs can be identified using either quantitative or qualitative research methods or a mixture of both. Market research companies and marketing departments often carry out customer surveys, with a range of closed to open questions. Both postal and a range of face-to-face approaches are used, such as those research questionnaires frequently to be found in shopping centres. While such an approach has the advantage of regularized and systematic

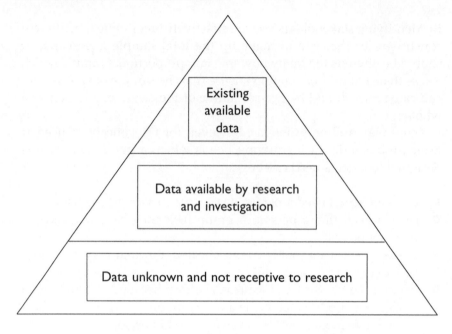

Figure 8.1   *Ease of availability of data*

data, problems arise when the organization wants to question the sample more thoroughly or in a much more focused way.

QUALITATIVE RESEARCH APPROACHES AND NEEDS IDENTIFICATION

To promote a more discursive approach to the identification of needs researchers eventually have to turn to more qualitative approaches. Common terms for such activities are market research and consumer trials. Whatever the focus and concern, the four main approaches in qualitative research are (Gorman and Clayton, 1997):

1. observation
2. interviewing
3. historical research
4. group discussion.

All of these are of potential value for decision making relating to the promotion of quality in goods and services. Historical research is also known in needs analysis as secondary market research, as it is concerned to interrogate existing data and information to assist in the design and delivery of decision-making processes.

A more common name in research for discussion groups is the term 'focus groups', which Krueger (1994) defines as:

a carefully planned discussion designed to obtain perceptions on a defined area of interest in a permissive, non-threatening environment. It is conducted (each time) with approximately 7 to 10 people by a skilled interviewer. The discussion is comfortable and often enjoyable for participants as they share their ideas and perceptions. Group members influence each other by responding to ideas and comments in the discussion. (p6)

Krueger adds that the purpose of a focus group is, through 'careful and systematic analysis of the discussions', to 'provide clues and insights as to how a product, service, or opportunity, is perceived' (Krueger, 1994, p6). While, therefore, focus groups are not the sole preserve of research into quality, they are a useful means of addressing quality issues, both in terms of product (the outcomes of a good or service or situation) and in terms of process, as we shall see later with action research for quality improvement.

Once the data about the needs of customers is collected, the research process is still not complete. The data has to be categorized (this is an example of . . .), collated, aggregated and analysed for implications in order to facilitate the decision making necessary to cater for those needs. In quality, this process is often called the development of the 'house of quality' or the more technical term 'quality function deployment' (QFD) (Munroe-Faure and Munroe-Faure, 1992). QFD can be defined as:

A technique or discipline for optimizing the process of developing and producing new products on the basis of customer need. (Kanji and Asher, 1996, p69)

The benefits of the technique is that it allows an analyst to bring together a variety of customer and stakeholder needs, requirements and priorities, with technical specifications and characteristics and competitor provision. For customer quality research and design purposes the 'house of quality' is a very flexible analytical instrument.

INTERNAL PROCESS CONTROL RESEARCH

The 'house of quality' is a technique used inside an organization. The design, control and management of internal processes is a central part of the TQM approach (Kanji and Asher, 1996). The significance of processes for quality and quality improvement is made by Cook (1996) who defines a quality process as:

> a series of steps or sequence of business activities the outcome of which is designed to achieve customer satisfaction by providing the customer with what they need, when they require it and in the manner in which they expect. (p2)

This definition does not distinguish between external and internal customers. This is an essential aspect of many quality developments, for 'customer satisfaction assessment for "internal" suppliers' (Jones, 1996) is a key part of process thinking for quality. For Cook, quality process thinking is:

> the generic term applied to improving an organization's effectiveness and efficiency by . . . (reviewing and) rethinking the way that business activities and processes are organized. (after pp2–3)

Quality process thinking and research coincide in a number of ways. Monitoring and evaluation research is a key part of management activity, while quality improvement is a key intention of action research (O'Hanlon, 1996) as well as collaborative inquiry (Reason, 1994). As all these items need to be addressed, the management cycle is dealt with first, before monitoring, evaluation and action research and action learning approaches are covered briefly.

The management cycle of activity

Simply put, the activity of management can be conceived of as a cycle of activity, typically with a series of interlocking activities as portrayed in Figure 8.2. Management is seen as involving four major sequential activities.

Despite the cyclical presentation of Figure 8.2, it is too often said that management begins with planning. The reality is that the activity of planning cannot be carried out without a minimum of understanding of the context and situation in which the management process is being carried out. These contexts can be external or internal to the organization and, whatever the contextual constraints and opportunities, an understanding of them is essential to the planning process. How can you plan without knowing the current state of affairs and the forces working for and against the manager and the successful accomplishment of the tasks and activities?

Figure 8.2 *The management cycle of activity*

For all of these reasons we consider that planning presupposes and requires at least a modicum of monitoring and evaluation. This is why, in our view, monitoring and evaluation is conceptually and practically a prerequisite to planning, and integral to its success. But what is meant by the terms monitoring and evaluation?

ACTIVITY

We have hinted at what monitoring and evaluation might be. We suggest that you now try to define what those terms mean, and what the differences are between them.

We have linked the two terms together on purpose, for they are closely linked. Both monitoring and evaluation involve a level of investigation (research) of the current state of affairs. There is, though, a key difference in the intentions of the two activities.

THE ESSENCE OF MONITORING AND EVALUATION RESEARCH

Monitoring can be a relatively simple process – that of 'keeping an eye on something'. The sort of monitoring we support is the more systematic process of examining, observing and overseeing. Monitoring is important, particularly in terms of checking whether or not any plans that were developed and are being implemented are actually being put into operation. In shorthand terms monitoring is checking whether or not what was intended to be done or implemented is actually occurring; it reviews the extent to which plans made are being implemented and expected results ensue.

The reality, of course, is that the best-laid plans often go awry. There can be a number of reasons for this, in addition to poor levels of planning – that contextual factors were not as they were thought to be, or that other forces came into play, or that the forces known at the outset to be at play were not as they were thought to be. Whatever the reality, the collection of data – whether it be qualitative or quantitative, small or large scale – is essential to the monitoring process.

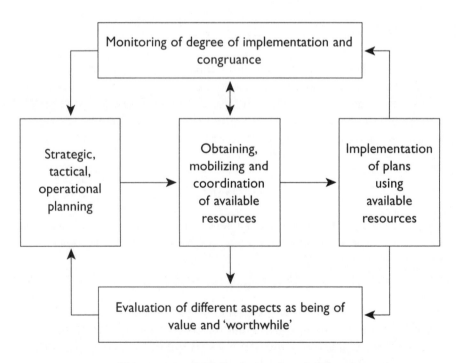

Figure 8.3 *Monitoring and evaluation*

The essence of evaluation

Evaluation is different from monitoring, though it often subsumes monitoring within it. Evaluation is the process of collecting and/or using information for the purposes of determining the value and worthwhileness of the subject of the evaluation process.

As Figure 8.3 shows, evaluation considers the worthwhileness (value) of something, while monitoring is the process of checking or verifying that what is intended is actually being put in place. In terms of Figure 8.3, monitoring identifies and reviews the degree of implementation and congruence of actuality with intention.

In arriving at decisions about the value and worthwhileness of an activity, Caldwell and Spinks (1988) provide the following useful equation of evaluation:

Evaluation = Quantitative descriptions
                   and/or   + Value judgements
                   Qualitative descriptions

The definition is useful, as it clearly highlights that evaluations can employ both qualitative and quantitative data collection methods. The subsequent analysis turns the data into information (used data) in order to reach a decision or view on the worthwhileness of the structures and processes being evaluated.

Caldwell and Spinks add two further distinctions, those of formative/ summative and major/minor evaluations. Formative evaluation is evaluation that is used to improve the processes under review (which is similar to the function of internal audits), while summative review is the process of appraising the overall effectiveness and outcomes of a programme or process (Caldwell and Spinks, 1988). Minor evaluations are defined as:

■ subjective in nature
■ concentrated on limited and focused data collection
■ short term
■ ongoing
■ resulting in single page reports.

On this basis, minor evaluations tend to be formative in nature; major evaluations tend to be the opposite of the minor characteristics, and are more akin to summative evaluations. In more colourful language, minor evaluations are often 'rough, fast and dirty', while major evaluations tend to be more sophisticated, measured and thorough.

Models of evaluation research

Not surprisingly there are many different approaches to evaluation, as well as to aspects of evaluation. Herman *et al.* (1987) provide a useful overview of the main approaches as part of the introduction of their 'evaluation kit' that comprises companion volumes in a series, and the following list is adapted from their work to show the most important models. (Full references to the different models are also provided by them before the different components of their own model is given.)

Model of evaluation	*Emphasis*
Goal oriented	Evaluation should assess progress and the effectiveness of outcomes.
Decision oriented	Evaluation feeds into intelligent and measured decision making.
Responsive (stakeholder)	Evaluation should depict programme processes and the value perspectives of key players.
Explanatory	Evaluation should focus on explaining effects, identifying causes of effects and generating generalizations about programme effectiveness.
Goal free	Evaluation should assess programme effects on alternative criteria and bases to those incorporated into the programme itself. Such effects are identified primarily by client research.
Advocacy-adversary	Evaluation should derive from the articulation and argumentation of contrasting points of view.
Utilization oriented	Evaluation concerned with the use of research findings on decision-making processes.

These different types of evaluation are not mutually exclusive, but overlap and complement each other. Whichever approach one uses it is important to be clear about what the purposes of the evaluation are. Indeed, Herman *et al.* see the clarification of the aims and parameters of the evaluation as being the first step in their model. The different but necessary processes in any evaluation, as they see it, are as follows.

Typical stages in an evaluation

Stage one   Establish the boundaries and focus of the evaluation (for whom, what, when, where, how).

Stage two   Select appropriate evaluation model and methods.

Stage three   Design the evaluation instruments and processes.

Stage four   Collect and analyse data.

Stage five   Report findings.

Within Herman *et al.*'s evaluation kit all of these stages are examined and explained in detail, as is the use and appropriateness of different research methods in the evaluation process. The major methodological distinction is that between qualitative and quantitative methods. It is helpful at this stage to review what the relative advantages and weaknesses of qualitative and quantitative approaches are.

ACTIVITY

In considering which research approach to use (qualitative or quantitative), what are the relative main benefits and weaknesses of each approach?

Completing the above activity might have proved difficult. If so, other chapters in this book are worth revisiting. In deciding which research methods to use the evaluator has to consider the advantages and weaknesses of the types of data provided by qualitative or quantitative methods as well as the specific context and nature of the evaluation. Patton (1987) summarizes their relative strengths and weaknesses as follows:

Qualitative methods permit the evaluator to study selected issues, cases or events in depth and detail; the fact that data collection is not constrained by predetermined categories of analysis contributes to the depth and detail of qualitative data. Quantitative methods, on the other hand, use standardized measures that fit diverse various opinions and experiences into predetermined response categories. The advantage of the quantitative approach is that it measures the reactions of a great many people to a limited set of questions, thus facilitating comparison and statistical aggregation of the data. This gives a broad, generalizable set of findings. By contrast, qualitative methods typically produce a wealth of detailed data about a much smaller number of people and cases. Qualitative data provide depth and detail.

On that basis, perhaps the most rounded approach is to utilize both sets of methodologies to provide standardization and insight. To review and confirm the differences, complete the following activity.

ACTIVITY

According to the quote from Patton, what are the strengths and weaknesses of qualitative and quantitative research methods?

Action research and quality improvement

The choice of title for this section was difficult, for there are a number of related and overlapping approaches, variously called action research, action learning, collaborative inquiry, practitioner research, reflective practice and action science (Schwandt, 1997).

One of the key aspects to be found in all of these approaches is that they are concerned with quality improvement and the 'transformation of organizations and communities towards greater effectiveness and greater justice' (Reason, 1994, p49). This transformation comes about by an emphasis on altering and improving processes, as shown in Figure 8.4.

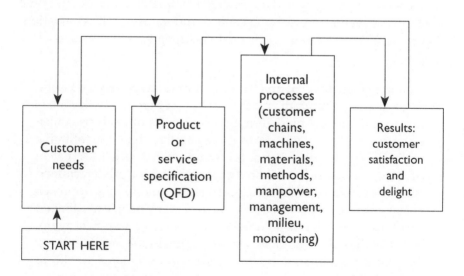

Figure 8.4 *Quality improvement processes*

According to Fuller and Petch (1995) action research thus is carried out as:

[a] planned series of stages incorporating a feedback loop in which the results of research inform the development of practice. (p199)

Zuber-Skerrett (1996) takes the concept of feedback loops and steps further by defining action research as:

collaborative, critical and self-critical inquiry by practitioners (eg teachers, managers) into a major problem or issue or concern in their own practice. They own and feel responsible and accountable for solving it through a cyclical process of:

1. strategic planning
2. action, ie implementing the plan
3. observation, evaluation and self-evaluation
4. critical and self-critical reflection on the results of points 1–3 and making decisions for the next cycle of action research, ie revising the plan, followed by action, observation and reflection, etc. (pp3–9)

Not surprisingly, the action research cycle adumbrated by Zuber-Skerrett is very close to the management cycle shown in Figure 8.2. Both aspects have a concern to improve quality and effectiveness of practical action within organizations. All the approaches contained in this chapter involve research, though in an eclectic fashion that tends to draw heavily (but not exclusively) on qualitative research methodologies. That still makes them research.

CONCLUSION

In this chapter monitoring has been defined as the process of checking whether what an organization actually does is what they intended to do. Evaluation, by extension, is the process of valuing or considering the worthwhileness of what an organization does. In particular, where there is a quality emphasis, this has become associated with a quality *improvement* perspective and emphasis.

On that basis, organizations that engage in monitoring, evaluation and quality improvement activities can claim to be on the way towards being a learning organization, ie one that, according to Garvin (1993):

is skilled at creating, acquiring and transferring knowledge, and at modifying its behaviour to reflect new knowledge and insights. (p80)

We hope you agree that the quote from Garvin sounds like a pretty good justification for considering monitoring, evaluation and quality improvement as legitimate research activities.

9

Reflections on the Research Process

Any piece of research should ideally also be a learning experience for the participants involved. Learning from the research process itself can enable constant self-improvement to occur; that is, when the opportunity arises to carry out research again, the researcher can build on previous experience, both good and bad! Consequently, the research design and research process should be better than previous attempts.

One of the most significant ways in which this learning can be achieved is through the processes of reflection (often called reflexivity or reflectivity (Schwandt, 1997). There are a number of ways and various points in a research programme when this reflection ought to take place. The main concern is that participants are given the opportunity to stop and think about the activities in which they are engaged.

AREAS FOR REFLECTION AND MEDITATION IN RESEARCH

There are many areas in research where reflection is invaluable, and in this section we address the most important.

The *aims* of the research project will need to be reviewed both initially and during the research process. There will be opportunities to revisit these aims at various points as the project proceeds. It is unusual for a research project to go exactly as planned.

The *methodology* will also need to be looked at. This aspect, of course, is necessary initially so as to ensure that the research methods chosen are fit for the purpose, and will provide the data that is required. As a project proceeds, it may be necessary to adjust the research methodologies. Ideally, of course, the piloting of research projects and methodologies should iron out any problems, such as the provision of inappropriate data, although that is not always the case. Reflection of the methodologies employed is also valuable when the research is complete. In particular, the researcher should ask whether or not the same results could have been achieved in a more satisfying or more cost-beneficial manner?

The *timescales* and *phases of the research project* should be reviewed. Research students who take 20 years to complete their PhD do not look good on the records of a university! It is possible that some slack may be built into the research process, but this should neither be assumed nor planned for. The researcher needs to be ruthless, as there is often much less flexibility built in than is required, particularly if the research is commissioned from external agencies such as research councils. Many grant-awarding bodies place time limits on both the completion of the research process and the submission of the necessary report; and students embarking on a research programme for a higher degree will find that they are required to complete their research within a reasonable period. As a result it is important to plan properly and systematically and to stick to schedules, though remaining open minded and flexible so as not to create further undue pressures if mishaps occur.

The *sample* size and stratified sample should also be kept under review. It is necessary to ensure that a sample size and sets of categories of respondents within the sample are as full and/or as representative as possible. Where the sample is not representative every opportunity for reflection and possible further action should be seized to ensure that every avenue has been explored, so that any shortcomings of the sample do not adversely affect the results and outcomes of the research. What this means, usually, is that the claims made for the research at the end are tempered by a degree of provisionality, even where the results cross-check and synchronize with the findings of other research projects.

The *results*, too, will need to be reflected upon. This reflection is usually carried out in two ways. The first is by the cross-examination and correlation of the results with other studies, both of the same kind and in the same area. If the results are similar, but the research methodologies of the studies were different, the results may be a case of triangulation – the cross-confirmation of findings from different perspectives.

Alternatively, if the results are significantly different from those of similar studies or of the same subject focus, consideration has to be given as to why this may be so. It may be that inadequate or inappropriate analysis of the data gives rise to different outcomes, or the other aspects of reflection that we mention in this chapter – such as sample size and characteristics – may be significant in generating different results. Whatever cross-confirmation occurs, the results have to be put in context. If the research project was collaborative as many of the collaborators as possible ought to be involved in the analysis of the results in order to promote if not assure the reliability of the findings.

The second way that the results are reflected upon is the strength of the claims made for them. Experience tells us that perfect samples and research instruments are seldom found. As a result, most research should be wary of universalism – the proposition that what was found was representative of the whole population under study. That may be the case, but without research that covers all the sample, is well planned, executed, analysed and presented, such universal claims should be seen as unrealistic, provisional and presumptuous.

An opportunity should also be taken to review the *ethics* of the research. The ethical considerations cover:

- the way access was gained to the research sample and situation
- the way(s) that data was collected, analysed and represented to the sample population
- the disclosure of data in any research report
- the nature of the outcomes and how they are reported and implications discussed.

Generally it is contended that it is immoral to attempt to dupe a sample in terms of research intentions, methodologies, analysis or disclosure of results and outcomes. That is, it is important for the researcher to have a clear moral framework to their research covering aspects such as care, trust and concern for the integrity and wishes of the respondents. Researching otherwise is manipulative and in bad faith. This is particularly the case in qualitative research, where the research process may be interlocutory, dialogical, collaborative and co-creative of understanding. All care should be taken to remain faithful to the sample and the context and to guard against the violation of their worth and credibility.

The *implications* of the research need to be considered carefully, and these mainly fall into three categories. First, harking back to the factors above, all researchers should ask themselves what lessons they have learned about carrying out the research, especially if they wish to attempt a similar project in the future. Second, the research needs to be considered for the contribution it makes to the sum of knowledge in an area. This can be both provisional and/or either confirmatory or disconfirmatory – supportive or critical of existing research findings and their implications for the topic. Third, there are likely to be implications about the direction that research in the area should take in the future.

Finally it is important to consider the philosophical *standpoint* of the researcher or research *vis à vis* the research. This aspect is considered in Chapter 11, and thus will not be dealt with here in detail. It is important to say, however, that discursive practice, the

> particular ways of talking and writing about and doing or performing one's practice that are coupled with particular social settings in which those ways of talking are regarded as understandable and more or less valuable (Schwandt, 1997, p31)

should be clearly articulated and understood. It is now accepted that the language used by researchers to define, analyse and understand their research practices and findings is socially and historically constructed. Researchers are to some extent the prisoners of their language and related ways of thinking (eg cause and effect, or mutual interaction and determination), so an awareness of these background, taken-for-granted assumptions is of great value to the researcher and others.

WHEN AND HOW TO REFLECT

Two further issues to be taken account of are *when* one should carry out the reflection and *how* it should be carried out. As we have indicated above, reflection can be carried out at any time. Reflections can be at a surface level (how it went today) or be deeper (how has what happened affected the research intentions, plan and outcomes?). Whatever the approach, reflection is probably most importantly conducted at the beginning and at the end of the research. These are the times when reflection can have most effect on the current project and on the direction which this research area as a whole should take.

Thus one can suggest that one axis of a graph should be:

Beginning reflection----Periodic formative review----End reflection

Second, one needs to consider how the reflective process can occur. It may be done *informally* by an *individual researcher* or by a *group of researchers*. Alternatively it may be a *more formal process*, in which the group attend a meeting to review the research. If this latter method is adopted, then the group should have a document such as an interim report (however imperfect) to work from. This gives all involved the opportunity to swap ideas and engage in a 'brainstorming' session which can be helpful to all concerned. These meetings need to be held regularly and be timetabled, since they may well end up being the only contact that collaborators have in what is undoubtedly a very busy world.

An alternative approach to the reflective process can be during the writing up of a *field journal* or *field notes*. The field is where events and social actions take place, irrespective of the presence or absence of the researcher. This is a naturalistic arena for research rather than an artificial setting such as laboratory experiments. A field journal is a notebook that the researcher carries into the field and in which they put comments and reflections as well as observational notes, snippets of conversation, ideas, lists, hypotheses, issues that arise and other helpful data and thoughts.

Consider too the extent to which respondents, at some point in the research, could be made part of this reflective process. This can be achieved either in the form of informal meetings or by correspondence when the research is completed.

A second axis of the graph might thus look something like the following:

Individual	Individual	Group	Group	Group/individual

informal--------formal--------formal--------informal--------mixed

Finally, a part of the process of reflection ought to involve some consideration of how the results of the research will be disseminated to the wider academic and social community. Dissemination might be in phases, or comprise a single event, be spoken or paper based. Whatever the approach, every attempt should be made to ensure that those interested in the research can gain access to it. This topic is dealt with more thoroughly in Chapter 11.

CONCLUSION

The process of reflection is a significant one for any committed researcher. Reflection is a multi-faceted phenomenon that is discussed in greater detail by McGill and Beaty (1992) and Schön (1983, 1987). What is important, as it is hoped that this chapter has shown, is that the reflection should be as comprehensive, analytical, specific and as positive as possible.

10

The Computer and Research

INTRODUCTION

The computer, particularly the personal computer (PC) desktop or laptop/portable has become a very useful aid for the researcher in recent years, and the PC is capable of fulfilling at least five functions:

- planning and completion of research contracts and projects
- collection and recording of data
- analysis of data
- presentation of data in different forms
- preparation for publication of the research.

In completing these, the researcher makes use of critical path planning and monitoring software, word processing, databases (including relational data bases), desktop publishing, spreadsheets, graphics facilities (including the facility for constructing charts) and specialized statistical and non-statistical data analysis software packages.

It is not our intention here to discuss all these capabilities in detail, as they are generally well known. There are excellent books, program manuals and on-line (Internet) support available from manufacturers, publishers and practitioners and/or researchers. As each function can be served by a number of different software packages, each with its own protocols, only a very general survey of such uses is possible, though suggestions for follow up are provided.

Qualitative researchers will have a particular requirement for word processing and prose analysis software. Any word processing package should have spelling, grammar checking and index-making facilities to support the coding and analysis of data. The facilities for cutting, pasting and copying are often an excellent way of conducting a preliminary analysis of qualitative data by allowing the researcher to collate data (eg of interviews) in different ways under different headings. In other words, the researcher can use the computer in ways similar to more 'traditional' uses not particularly connected with research.

An alternative use of computers in research is in the processing of quantitative data. To do this effectively the researcher does need to think carefully about how the data is to be stored initially. This will save time later, and storing the data in the form required eliminates the need for retyping or translation before processing. This will normally mean using a standard spreadsheet package (such as Excel) to store data, from where it can be exported directly into a statistical package and processed without further ado. The researcher might consider using optical mark or bar code readers (eg from precoded questionnaires) to feed in data. This might seem troublesome to set up but such procedures can save time in data collection and processing.

THE COMPUTER AND QUANTITATIVE DATA

A variety of computer-based statistical packages are available for the analysis of quantitative data. Packages such as MINITAB, SPSS and SAS cover most of the basic and more advanced requirements of researchers, and guides to their use are available from the manufacturers and commercial publishers. Additionally, they are very user friendly with excellent 'Help' facilities. What the packages do not always do, however, is inform the user if the particular data analysis technique they are about to use is the most appropriate or correct one. Consequently, the sort of data the researcher has and the nature of its distribution are still themes that need to be confronted.

If you intend to use one of these packages make sure that:

- the package(s) are readily available
- the package(s) are compatible with the computer being used
- the appropriateness of any techniques being used is understood (and can be justified to other researchers)
- you are in a position to present data to the computer in a usable form (eg on an appropriate spreadsheet).

Below are some of the standard statistical packages.

Package	Description
Minitab	Basic statistical package with some arithmetic functions and exploratory data analysis
SPSS SAS Genstat	General purpose statistical packages with a wide range of elementary and advanced statistics
Glim	A useful modelling package
Lisrel	This package is particularly useful for path analysis and the analysis of structural models
ML3/MLn	A multi-level modelling package
CMU-DAP	Useful for exploratory data analysis
SCICONIC	A useful package for linear and non-linear programming.

It is sometimes possible for researchers attached to research institutions to have packages installed on their own computers at home for ease of use, depending on the precise form of licence that an institution has with the software supplier. If it is planned to install software purchased by an institution on a personal computer, be sure to check that doing so will not infringe copyright.

Data is imported into a package, after which selection occurs from a menu of the statistical test (correlations, factor analysis, etc) that the researcher wishes to use. In these broad areas further choices are usually available with more advanced statistics. If choices are not expressed, a default setting may be selected by the program. It is thus very important to be fully aware of how the package approaches and then progresses an analysis. Some packages (MINITAB is a good example) provide considerable flexibility for reorganizing data in the process.

With the 'general purpose' packages it is usually possible to try different methods of analysis. If a factor analysis is being attempted, it may well be that an initial analysis with a varimax rotation does not provide clean factors. If so, the researcher may wish to return to the analysis and repeat it using, for instance, an oblimax.

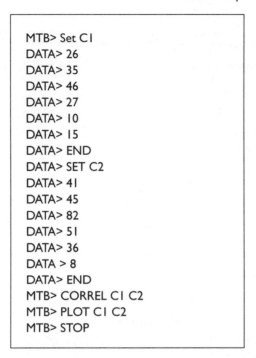

```
MTB> Set C1
DATA> 26
DATA> 35
DATA> 46
DATA> 27
DATA> 10
DATA> 15
DATA> END
DATA> SET C2
DATA> 41
DATA> 45
DATA> 82
DATA> 51
DATA> 36
DATA > 8
DATA> END
MTB> CORREL C1 C2
MTB> PLOT C1 C2
MTB> STOP
```

Figure 9.1 *Using MINITAB to calculate a Pearson product moment correlation coefficient*

In the program shown in Figure 9.1 two columns (C1, C2) contain the data from two variables. The computer is able to calculate the correlation coefficient and provide a graphical plot of the correlation so the data can be presented and reviewed in different formats. By way of contrast, the same calculation using SPSS would require instructions like those shown in Figure 9.2. It should be noted that the precise format of such calculations can change, depending on the type of package and the computer hardware used.

Some of the packages have more specialist applications. While researchers can undertake some modelling with general purpose packages it is much better if a specialist software package such as GLIM is available. Similarly, MLn is a specialist package available specifically for multi-level modelling. The specialist facility LISREL is available as an 'add-on' for SPSS.

THE COMPUTER AND QUALITATIVE DATA

Though not usually required to the same level of numerical sophistication as quantitative data analysis, there are a number of packages

```
Read Data ★
Data List ★
Fixed ★
Num Var ★
[Alt] [T]
VI 1-2V2 3-4
Read or Write Data ★
Begin Data ★
2641 ★
3545 ★
4682 ★
2751 ★
1036 ★
1508 ★
[Esc]
[Alt] [E]
Main Menu
Analyse Data ★
Correlation and Regression ★
Correlation ★
Variables ★
[Alt] [T]
VI V2 ★
Read or Write Data ★
Save ★
[Alt] [M]
■ ◇
FI0 ★
```

Figure 9.2 *Calculation of correlation coefficient using SPSS*

available for the analysis of qualitative data. Qualitative analysis is somewhat more difficult because such data by its very nature is unlikely to be presented in simple response (eg yes/no) formats. Different levels of sophistication of analysis, however, are still available.

At the simplest level a great deal of analysis can be done using the capabilities of word processing programs such as Microsoft Word. Once the data is available in transcript form it is possible, using the 'cut and paste' facilities, to effect an analysis of qualitative data. As well as analysing transcripts in totality in terms of their answers, and in comparison with each other, answers from different respondents to the same question can be grouped together and analysed. Similarly, it is possible to collate together and separately the responses of different categories of respondents (eg by age, gender, occupation) to identify similarities and differences in response by those (independent) variables. It is possible also to use the 'find' facility of word processing programs to search any number of transcripts for key words or sets of words of significance to the research. For many researchers this approach using word processing program capabilities is all that will be required for the analysis.

More sophisticated capabilities are offered by the qualitative data analysis packages currently available, some of which are Hypersoft, Ethnograph and NUD.IST (Non-numerical Unstructured Data by Indexing, Searching and Theorizing).

In these programs the qualitative data can be analysed, reordered and collated by the use of descriptive and axial coding approaches. The specialist programs also allow for the speculative ordering of data, and the creation of stem diagrams and links showing the connections of arguments and positions across and within qualitative data. No statistical tests of significance are available as such, but this is of little consequence, for the rationale for qualitative data in the first place is its richness and openness. Instead, the significance is shown by the ways the data is analysed, chopped up, re-ordered and re-presented, and links made to existing literature and research. The computer has still to be fully exploited in these processes.

GETTING INFORMATION VIA THE COMPUTER

Researchers are increasingly using the Internet and e-mail for:

- data collection (eg computer surveys or secondary data use)
- research collaborations and communication
- professional research associations
- research publications, especially ongoing and preliminary publications.

As research and other journals are increasingly being published on the Internet (on-line) greater amounts of research are being published electronically. It is possible to obtain articles electronically as well, though this may require specialist reader programs (eg Adobe Acrobat) as well as fees. One example of a very valuable initiative in this area is the British Education Index Education-Line initiative. Based at the Brotherton Library of the University of Leeds with the e-mail address education-line@leeds.ac.uk it links researchers and authors with an accessible database where they can read publications and place their own if they so desire. The emphasis of this particular scheme is with 'grey' working or otherwise unpublished materials rather than finished articles or research.

Many university, college and national libraries now allow their catalogues to be accessed via the Internet. It is possible (sometimes with the payment of a registration fee) to refer to the catalogues and confirm the presence and location of books and journals before having to undertake what might have been a fruitless journey. Do be aware, however, that many libraries have not placed all their materials on-line. This applies particularly to older books and journals. It may still be necessary (particularly for those undertaking historical studies) to have access to original catalogues.

THE COMPUTER AND THE CONSTRUCTION OF FINAL RESEARCH REPORTS

The computer is also very valuable in the production of final reports, articles and books. Almost without exception, some revision will be necessary, perhaps because of criticism (friendly or otherwise) from friends, colleagues and referees. It is therefore very important to be able to revise and update research materials. This, of course, is where access to a good quality word processor is essential. While most word processing software offer graphics and desktop publishing capabilities, specialist software is valuable in areas such as:

- charts and tables (often using spreadsheets)
- graphics
- desktop publishing.

Software such as CORELflow enables a writer to construct charts and flow diagrams and import these into a text. This is very easy to do and can add considerable clarity to a document. Graphics software is very useful for preparing tables, graphs and pie charts. Desktop publishing software is also invaluable where it is required to reformat text and produce it in unusual formats such as page layouts using columns. Journal and book publishers usually produce guidelines to assist potential authors (see Chapter 11). Scanners and the associated software are useful for importing photographs or diagrams into a text provided copyright is not infringed.

OTHER COMPUTER USES AND SOURCES

Project planning software (eg MacProject) that allows for time and task date charts might be of some value to the researcher. Another useful type of software is accounting software packages, say if the researcher is undertaking contract research and needs to be accountable for income and expenditure. It is particularly useful if a project combines different funding sources, as budget lines can be dedicated to specific and identifiable costs such as travel, subsistence and secretarial, and provide regular interim as well as final accounts.

For complex multi-level or multi-method research projects packages such as MINITAB contain some elementary mathematical functions, though software packages such as Mathcad, Mathematica and Axiom take this much further if required. Numerous directories of software (eg the *Chest Software Directory* in the UK) are published each year, and provide excellent overviews and descriptions of available packages, many of which are available for trial and practice (usually with save-disabled, ie it is not possible to save and store files).

Suitable computer hardware capability is of course required. The researcher should seek as much RAM (accessible, usable memory) and storage capability as possible, for these can allow the simultaneous use of multiple computer programs as well as extensive data storage (but remember to copy on to floppy disks). In addition a printer is needed (of at least the bubble jet type) for drafting and final presentation. Other useful facilities are access to a scanner, a link to the Internet and, possibly, optical mark reading machines.

The computer can, however, only deliver what it is programmed to do. There is always the possibility of 'rubbish in, rubbish out'. In this sense, the computer is only a useful adjunct to the research. It is no substitute or ameliorative for a well-designed, well-planned and well-executed research project.

11

Writing the Final Report and Getting the Work Published

While there is always a personal involvement in research, its value lies in the communication of the results and conclusions to a wider audience. This is true whether the outcome is a conference paper, an article for a scholarly or professional journal, a book or part of a book, a report or a thesis/dissertation.

The intended audience is an important factor in determining the form and structure of any research report. In a piece of applied research, such as an evaluation commissioned by clients whose main interest is in the recommendations, a final report might emphasize the conclusions and recommendations and place comparatively less emphasis on theoretical and methodological details. Research conducted for a higher degree will have a different structure, where the examiners will be interested in the appropriateness of the methodology employed, the data collecting and analysis methods used, what decisions needed to be made and so on. There will therefore be a need to highlight these issues in the final document. It is thus necessary at a fairly early stage of the research to identify the target audience and find out and clarify their expectations of the final document.

Writing needs to start at an early point in the research process. Any research document, whether it be a thesis, a report or some other type of communication, will be written and rewritten several times before submission. Starting early also provides the researcher with the opportunity to keep the whole research process under review, along with its progress and any alterations necessary. It is far easier to edit something than to write it in the first place. Do not worry about style or getting the content exactly right – that can be done later.

Early writing also serves a useful psychological purpose. It provides the writer with the confidence that 'something' has been achieved. Even if it is going to be rewritten and improved several times the researcher has at least got something under his or her belt. Indeed, the longer the writing process is delayed the more difficult it becomes to start at all. This may mean that early drafts are incomplete and stylistically naive, or that some sections are present only as titles. This is not important, for early writing begins to define the structure of the final article.

It is also a valuable exercise to report on research at seminars and conferences. An invitation to speak at a conference is both confidence building and an opportunity to gain valuable feedback from the audience about the current state of the research and possible directions in which it could proceed. Presentations force the researcher to reflect on and then construct a suitable presentation. This in itself is an extremely useful exercise.

STARTING A REPORT

Before starting work on any report, examine how others have approached this task – look at a typical article, thesis or research report. The successful ones are usually fairly readily available at universities and other libraries. If a thesis is on library shelves it usually means that it has earned the writer the degree sought. In other words, it has been successful. This does not mean of course that a thesis does not contain faults or cannot be improved, but that it was deemed sufficient.

If the research is in a specific subject the researcher should search the Aslib *Index to Theses* (or *Dissertation Abstracts* if it was produced for an American or Canadian university). The Aslib *Index* gives, in chronological order, the titles of all MPhil and PhD theses successfully submitted to UK universities, classified according to subject area. They may be obtainable via the inter-library loan system; and availability is growing with microfiche and other storage methods.

Alternatively, the researcher should look at articles on the topic area in a quality (ie refereed) journal. This can provide a template on how to tackle an article for a learned journal.

TIP

If you have a specific journal in mind for possible placement of an article, check the journal for their own house style, methods of presenting data and literature referencing. Usually the requirements are summarized in the journal itself or in detailed notes from the journal editor(s). Examine the section labelled 'Notes for Authors'.

The particular points to note when you are examining an article or thesis are the following.

- *Overall length of the article* Due to space restrictions, many editors are careful to limit the number of words in an article.
- *How should the report be written?* Reports can be written chronologically (this was done first, followed by . . .), to tell a particular story (eg a case study), thematically, or in terms of some logical structure.
- *Amount of space allocated to the various components of the article* Writings have to be balanced, or slanted towards the particular concerns of a journal. Check how long is the literature survey, the space devoted to methodology and to conclusions (as well as what is in those sections).
- *The manner in which different parts of the article are interrelated* How is the literature survey structured and related to the research questions and the methodology? How are the final conclusions related back to the literature survey? Have the research questions been confirmed or been modified in the light of the research?
- *What does the article contain that is 'new' and/or original?* The concept of 'originality' is discussed later in this chapter, but any article/thesis ought to contain novel (original) materials. Existing materials could be evaluated in a new way or extended in some way (eg new data or a different sample from those researched previously). Methodology and/or data collecting instruments may be new developments or entirely new, or new theoretical structures proposed or existing theoretical structures modified in the light of this new data. The researcher should exploit the interest of editors in novelty.
- *What are the main conclusions?* When assertions are made, editors are entitled to ask 'Who says so?' and 'What is their evidence or rationale for those assertions?'
- *What is the function of the report?* The purpose of an article/report determines the overall strategy of construction. If the report is to be submitted as a thesis or dissertation for a higher degree then the examiners will require a complete picture of the research project (how the research was conducted, what data was collected, how the researcher arrived at the conclusions, etc). Alternatively, if the research was commissioned, the audience may well be less interested in the methodology adopted than in the results. In the latter case it might be more prudent to put the main findings and recommendations first, and include other materials in appropriate appendices.

Having made a decision about these strategic matters it should be possible to map out section or chapter headings for the whole report. While it is difficult to prescribe the order of topics and the detail required it is possible to indicate typical areas of the research which should be included and described in the report.

ORIGINALITY

An important concept underlying any article, thesis, book or conference presentation is that of originality. Editors particularly are keen to publish something that is new or original. Originality can be demonstrated by new:

- Methodologies
- Tools and/or techniques
- Area of research
- Knowledge and/or outcomes
- Use of data
- Interpretations of existing material
- Theory or modification of existing theory
- Application of existing theory to new areas
- Synthesis of ideas
- Evidence about an old issue
- Data obtained from new, different sample

Simply having 'new data' will not necessarily constitute original material. In a good piece of research the conclusions will seek to assess the strengths and weaknesses of any theoretical approaches employed by linking the data to the constructs and variables used in the theory.

THE OVERALL STRUCTURE OF THE REPORT

What follows is a list of possible contents for a report, article or thesis – it is not suggested that everything in the list be included. The list should be used as a check during and at the conclusion of writing so that obvious omissions can be corrected before publication. In addition, the different sections need not necessarily be in the order given below.

- Title
- Acknowledgements
- Abstract

- Contents
- Introduction
- Literature review
- Research questions/aims/hypotheses
- Methodology
- Data collecting methods
- Data
- Data analysis methods
- Discussion
- Conclusions
- Reflection
- References
- Bibliography
- Appendices
- Miscellaneous additions

Some of the items do not require much further discussion.

The title should be an accurate reflection of what the work is about. Be precise without being overlong. Contributions of other people (eg supervisors, partners) should be acknowledged, except where any requirements of confidence would be breached. The abstract should be brief but accurate. Typically, an abstract states:

- what the topic is
- how it was researched
- what the main conclusions are.

An introduction should essentially 'set the scene'. It needs to briefly place the problem studied in context and indicate why it is/was an issue worthy of research. An introduction also provides a guide to the overall report (what is covered where) for readers – a sort of advance organizer.

Some indication of seminal literature may be included in the introduction, but the substantive literature survey is normally the next section. While there are a number of purposes behind conducting a literature survey the most important is the indication it gives of the current state of knowledge and theoretical understanding of the problem being investigated.

It is necessary to decide just how wide to cast the net when constructing a literature survey. Key words or concepts drawn from a thesaurus can help here, though there are no absolute rules. Some writers concentrate on the issue at hand and omit materials they consider peripheral; others take a broader view and context. Deciding which strategy to adopt will partly depend on how well the particular topic has been researched. Generally, the more it has been researched, the tighter should be the focus.

It is vital, however, to ensure that the most significant recent sources are included. The researcher ought to look at recent books, journal articles, abstracts, conference proceedings and theses (possibly patent literature in some cases) at the outset. Where the topic is novel (little previous research reported) the researcher may have to go further back in time and look for contiguous sources that can be drawn upon in the construction of the research questions and design. Current theoretical positions should be identified in the literature survey, as should specific technical terms, particularly those that are contentious (eg 'gifted' or 'professional'). Most importantly, however, the literature review should be relevant and up to date.

Any research questions will need to be included and discussed. These should be related to the literature survey and the approaches to data collection (eg sampling and sample size) and analysis. The methodology needs to be explained and justified in terms of suitability and operationalization. Specific data collecting techniques should be discussed and justified with issues of reliability and validity dealt with.

An analysis of all data (qualitative and/or quantitative) is presented in the data analysis section. Data should be presented for easy use and reference by the reader, with care being taken to ensure that the presentation is not marred by the researcher's long acquaintance with it. If there are large amounts of data (such as interview transcripts) then it may be necessary to place it in an appendix or even a separate document. The methods of analysis used will need to be justified and explained with examples provided. This is particularly the case with qualitative data, where practitioners may have developed their own codings and data analysis methods.

The final three sections (Discussion, Conclusions, Reflection) are often combined. The discussion typically deals with both the extent to which any research questions have been answered by the piece of research and how it contributes to relevant theory and literature. Issues that can arise include:

- the extent to which relevant theory has been proved, disproved or modified and extended in the light of the research
- the extent to which the writings of key authors have to be amended, extended or abandoned
- the extent to which new theories, approaches or insights have been produced and validated.

Shortcomings of the research (if any!) are best presented here, as are recommendations for further work and action in the light of the research. Future research possibilities and requirements should be adumbrated, as should possible implications for any changes in professional roles and practice. The researcher should not be shy at this stage, but neither should they be overly boastful.

In addition it is useful to reflect on the research. If it were to be conducted again what would change? How could the research be done differently? Every piece of research should not only be a process of discovery but also a learning experience for the researcher.

To support the writing up process further, see Cummings and Frost (1995) and Mullins (1977), who cover the area of writing for scholarly journals and the more general issue of publication in greater detail.

THE COMPLETION OF THE REPORT WRITING PROCESS

The process of producing a report, thesis or book requires careful management and planning. Many aspects are time consuming rather than difficult. It is essential, for instance, that the format of the report is correct and conforms to any rubrics available. Publishers and universities usually give fairly precise details about how the material should be presented, such as:

- spacing in text and size of margins
- presentation methods for tables and diagrams
- binding and titling arrangements
- number and size of copies required (eg A4, A5, etc)
- whether paper-based manuscript and/or disc should be submitted.

The researcher needs to be aware of these requirements and to follow them as closely as possible. Checking for spelling, grammar and typing errors are invariably the responsibility of the author, both initially and at any proofing or final presentation stages.

VIVA VOCES OF RESEARCH FOR HIGHER DEGREES

Since most higher degrees by research require some sort of viva before the degree will be awarded it is useful for someone (possibly the supervisor) to provide a 'mock viva' so as to acclimatize the candidate to the examination situation.

Setting up the examination system will be the responsibility of the university. Supervisors play an important part here, for it is they who tend to have knowledge of other researchers in the field. Candidates should normally expect at least two examiners, one of whom will be external to the organization and therefore possibly not known to candidates personally. The internal examiner may be the candidate's own supervisor, although some university regulations forbid this. Examiners are required to be experienced in researching and examining in the subject area. Candidates would do well to know of the work of their external examiners but are usually forbidden from having any contact with them before an examination.

Supervisors and those responsible for setting up the examination arrangements need to start this process well in advance. Many universities indicate in their regulations the period of notice that is required from approval of arrangements to the time when the actual examination can occur. It is essential to comply with such regulations, for not to do so can cause irritation and unnecessary stress.

The precise form of the viva voce varies, making it impossible to predict what questions will be asked. Typically, however, candidates are expected to defend their thesis and explain and justify the approach used. Examiner questions might include:

- *General 'global' questions* Why the interest in this area? Why a particular methodology? What are the professional and/or social implications of the research?
- *Questions relating to the methodology* How were any research questions developed? How and why were the research methods and techniques chosen? Why a particular sample? What are the advantages of the data analysis methods?
- *Specific questions* Why were particular theoretical frameworks or concepts chosen? Why was a chart presented in a particular way?
- *Questions related to perceived strengths and weaknesses of the research.*
- *Questions which invite the candidate to be self-critical* What alternative approaches were considered and decided against? What possible alternative methods of approaching the problem are there? What would be done the same and/or differently were the research to be carried out again?

PUBLISHING

Researchers may wish to have their work published or at least disseminated to a wider audience than that normally available to a thesis. There are four widely used avenues for this process.

1. *Publication as a chapter or whole book* It is usual for editors of collections to approach possible contributors, while intending book authors normally approach a publisher to discuss publication. If successful, a contract is usually drawn up covering time-scales and guidelines.
2. *Presentation of research at a conference* Research societies and professional bodies usually provide and promote conferences which can be useful to attend even if the research is in progress. The discussion which follows the presentation of a paper can be very valuable feedback for the researcher. Conference proceedings are sometimes published, either in a house journal or in book form; they may be refereed or non-refereed.
3. *Publication in a scholarly journal* As with books, it is important to locate a suitable journal, one that publishes in the research area or that specializes in the style of the researcher (eg action research journals). When a suitable journal is found it is essential that the potential author examines the notes for intending authors that give details of presentation methods, format of graphs and diagrams, etc, and these notes should be followed.
4. *Publication in house* These are often less prestigious than outside publishers, but they do serve the purpose of bringing new practitioner or student work to an audience, albeit normally rather a small one. To maximize the effectiveness of such a body it is important they have an editorial board – to vet submissions, to provide ISBN numbers so that the works appear in the appropriate bibliographies, and to ensure that desktop publishing and binding facilities are readily available.

References to assist book publication

Intending British authors should refer to books such as the *Writers' and Artists' Yearbook* (A and C Black) or *The Writer's Handbook* (Macmillan), while North American writers need volumes such as *Writer's Market* (World Digest Books) or *Publisher's Trade List Annual* (a set of publishers' catalogues). In addition bibliographies such as *Books in Print* (Whitaker) in the UK or *Books in Print* (Bowker) in the USA contain details of publishers. Contact individual publishers who publish in your researcher area, but be prepared to suffer a number of refusals. Books need to be saleable and some pieces of research, however interesting they may be to the writer, and however well the research might have been carried out, are not necessarily of interest to a wide number of readers. A refusal to publish, therefore, is in no sense a reflection on the quality of the work.

References to assist journal publication

American journals in education are listed in Cabell's *Directory of Publishing Opportunities in Education*, while UK journals tend to be listed in UK abstracting journals (eg *Technical Education and Training Abstracts* from Carfax), which provide a list at the end of the journals that are abstracted.

Articles for journals are usually vetted. Various methods are used, depending on the journal, including:

- double blind refereeing (two referees with authors unknown)
- single blind refereeing (one referee with authors unknown)
- editorial/advisory boards (that may employ 'blind' referees)
- vetting by an editor.

It is important not be depressed by refusal, while revisions are often required even where an article is accepted for publication. The time taken for the article to appear can be quite long, as there is considerable pressure for space in the more prestigious journals. Authors typically are asked to check proofs of articles before printing. As it is difficult and expensive to make major changes at or after this point it is essential that the article is 'right' first time.

References and bibliographies are normally presented using the Harvard system (see Chapter 6). As there can be variations, it is important to check carefully that the intended style of presentation is acceptable.

CONCLUSION

For many researchers the construction of the final report is one of the most rewarding parts of the process. Often it is only at this point that the full implications of what has been done and achieved become apparent. Although the constant checking and rechecking of text and figures can be tiresome, one can obtain a real sense of achievement from the overall process.

When the research is finally completed and the report/publication is written, what happens next? While it may be necessary to have a rest, or re-establish contact with partners and friends, it can be important to maintain the research momentum. The completion of a successful research project can be a useful springboard for gaining further or new funds, for previous publications (a 'track record') are an important criterion for funding agencies.

What may be necessary also is the development and maintenance of a 'research culture' within an organization. This can be very difficult, particularly when there are other worthwhile activities competing for both funding and time. There are however a number of ways to foster such a culture:

1. management who are sympathetic to, and supportive of research
2. hosting research seminars and conferences at regular intervals (both in house and through professional associations)
3. a physical centre such as a research unit where help and advice, particularly with publications, are available
4. a structure (departmental research committees, etc) which can help to promote research activity
5. by it being made obvious to all staff that research is important and recognized.

Many researchers do end up feeling dissatisfied with what they have done, despite the many associated achievements that may have occurred. Doing the research better or in a different way, or moving on to other research issues and topics, often become a preoccupation. Done properly, with enough time and resources, research can be life enhancing, exhilarating and taxing all at the same time. Research can be addictive! If it is, do not try to fight it, but do attempt to keep a balance between the different aspects and demands on your time and obligations.

References

Abramson, M (ed) (1996) *Further and Higher Education Partnerships: The future for collaboration*, Open University Press, Buckingham.

Adelman, C (1993) 'Kurt Lewin and the origins of action research', *Educational Action Research*, **1** 1, pp1–20.

Alreck, P L and Settle, R B (1985), *The Survey Research Handbook*, Irwin, Homewood, ILL.

Anastasi, A (1988) *Psychological Testing*, Collier-Macmillan, New York.

Anderson, G (1990) *Fundamentals of Educational Research*, Falmer Press.

Barzun, J and Graff, H F (1992) *The Modern Researcher*, Harcourt, Brace, San Diego.

Bell, J (1993) *Doing Your Research Project*, Open University Press, Buckingham.

Bennett, R (1992) *Dictionary of Personnel and Human Resources Management*, Pitman, London.

Bennis,W, Parikh, B and Lessem, R (1994) *Beyond Leadership*, Macmillan, London.

Blalock, H M (1981) *Social Statistics*, McGraw-Hill, Maidenhead.

Bliss, J, Monk, M and Ogborn, J (1983) *Qualitative Data Analysis for Educational Research*, Croom Helm, London.

Bolman, L G and Deal, T E (1984) *Modern Approaches to Understanding and Managing Organizations*, Jossey-Bass, London.

Burgess, R G (1989) *The Ethics of Educational Research*, Falmer Press, Lewes.

Buros, O K (1978) *The Eighth Mental Measurements Yearbook*, Buros Institute of Mental Measurements, Lincoln, NE.

Caldwell, B J and Spinks, J M (1988) *The Self-managing School*, Falmer Press, Lewes.

Campbell, D T and Stanley, J C (1966) *Experimental and Quasi-experimental Designs for Research*, Rand McNally, Chicago.

Campbell-Kease, J (1989) *A Companion to Local History Research*, A and C Black, London.

Carmines, E G and Zeller, R A (1979) *Reliability and Validity Assessment*, Sage, London.

Carr, W and Kemmis, S (1986) *Becoming Critical*, Falmer Press, Lewes.

Cassell, C and Symon, G (eds) (1994) *Qualitative Methods in Organisational Research: A Practical Guide*, London: Sage

Child, D (1990) *Factor Analysis*, Holt, London.

Clegg, S R (1989) *Frameworks of Power*, Sage, London.

Cochran, W G (1977) *Sampling Techniques*, Wiley, Chichester.

Cohen, L and Manion, L (1994) *Research Methods in Education*, Routledge, London.

Cook, S (1996) *Process Improvement: A handbook for managers*, Gower, Aldershot.

Coulthard, L J (1985) *An Introduction to Discourse Analysis*, Longman, Harlow.

Croll, P (1986) *Systematic Classroom Observation*, Falmer Press, Lewes.

Cummings, L L and Frost, P J (eds) (1995) *Publishing in the Organizational Sciences*, Sage, London.

Czarniawska, B and Sevon, G (eds) (1996) *Translating Organizational Change*, De Gruyter, Berlin.

Dale, B G and Plunkett, D (1995) *Quality Costing* (2nd edn), Chapman & Hall, London.

Dawson, S (1992) *Analysing Organisations* (2nd edn), Macmillan, London.

Dey, I (1993) *Qualitative Data Analysis*, Routledge, London.

Doherty, G D (ed) (1994) *Developing Quality Systems in Education*, Routledge, London.

Drever, E (1995) *Using Semi-structured Interviews in Small-scale research*, Scottish Council for Research in Education, Edinburgh.

Edwards, A D and Westgate, D P G (1994) *Investigating Classroom Talk*, Falmer Press, Lewes.

Elliott, J (1991) *Action Research for Educational Change*, Open University Press, Buckingham.

Ericsson, K A and Simon, H A (1993) *Protocol Analysis*, MIT Press, Cambridge, MA.

Etzioni, A (1964) *Complex Organizations*, Holt, Rinehart & Winston, New York.

Evans, R J (1995) 'Quality versus cost – Lessons from the late 1990s', *Managing Service Quality*, **5**, 1 pp6–101wx.

Everett, B (1980) *Cluster Analysis*, Gower, Aldershot.

Fetterman, D M (1989) *Ethnography*, Sage, London.

Fitz-Gibbon, C T and Morris, L L (1987) *How to Design a Programme Evaluation*, Sage, London.

Fletcher, C L (1996) *Exploring Tracer Studies: A review and a case study*, Education Research Unit, Wolverhampton University.

Flynn, N (1997) *Public Sector Management* (3rd edn) Prentice Hall, Hemel Hempstead.

Foster, P (1996) *Observing Schools*, Chapman, London.

Foucault, M (1977) *Discipline and Punish: The birth of the prison*, Penguin, Harmondsworth.

Fransella, F and Bannister, D (1977) *A Manual for Repertory Grid Techniques*, Academic Press, London.

Fuller, R and Petch, A (1995) *Practitioner Research*, Open University Press, Buckingham.

Garvin, D A (1993) 'Building a Learning Organization', *Harvard Business Review*, **71** July–August, p80.

Goffman, E (1961) *Asylums*, Penguin, Harmondsworth.

Gordon, J R (1993) *A Diagnostic Approach to Organizational Behavior*, Allyn & Bacon, Newton, MA.

Gorman, G E and Clayton, P (1997) *Qualitative Research for the Information Professional*, Library Association, London.

Green, D E and Tull, D (1978) *Research for Marketing Decisions*, Prentice Hall, Hemel Hempstead.

Greene, J and D'Oliveira, M (1982) *Learning to Use Statistical Tests in Psychology*, Open University Press, Buckingham.

Guest, D E (1990) 'Human resource management and the American dream', *Journal of Management Studies*, **27** 4, pp377–97.

Guilford, J P (1954) *Psychometric Methods*, McGraw-Hill, Maidenhead.

Guilford, J P and Fruchter, B (1979) *Fundamental Statistics in Psychology and Education*, McGraw-Hill, Maidenhead.

Hammersley, M and Atkinson, P (1983) *Ethnography: Principles in practice*, Routledge, London.

Hargreaves, A (1978) 'The significance of classroom coping strategies', in Barton, L and Meighan, R (eds) *Sociological Interpretations of Schooling and Classrooms: A Reappraisal*, Nafferton Books, Driffield, pp73–100.

Hatch, J A and Wisniewski, R (eds) (1995) *Life History and Narrative*, Falmer Press.

Herman, J L, Morris, L L and Fitz-Gibbon, C T (1987) *Evaluator's Handbook*, Sage, London.

Hitchcock, G and Hughes, A (1995) *Research and the Teacher*, Routledge, London.

Hodkinson, P, Sparkes, A C and Hodkinson, H (1996) *Trumphs and Tears: Young people, markets and the transition from school to work*, David Fulton, London.

Hopkins, D (1989) *Evaluation for School Development*, Open University Press, Buckingham.

Howard, K and Sharpe, J A (1983) *The Management of a Student Research Project*, Gower, Aldershot.

Jackson, C (1996) *Understanding Psychological Testing*, British Psychological Society, Leicester.

Jones, C R (1996) 'Customer satisfaction assessment for "Internal" Suppliers', *Managing Service Quality*, **6** 1, pp45–48.

Jorgensen, D L (1989) *Participant Observation: A methodology for human sciences*, Sage, London.

Kanji, G K and Asher, M (1996) *100 Methods for Total Quality Management*, Sage, London.

Kendall, M G (1970) *Rank Correlation Methods*, Griffin, London.

Kirk, J and Miller, M L C (1986) *Reliability and Validity in Qualitative Research*, Sage, London.

Kish, L (1965) *Survey Sampling*, Wiley, Chichester.

Kitson Clark, G (1968) *Guide for Research Students Working on Historical Subjects*, Cambridge University Press.

Klecka, W R (1980) *Discriminant Analysis*, Sage, London.

Kline, P (1994) *An Easy Guide to Factor Analysis*, Routledge, London.

Kline, P (1993) *A Handbook of Psychological Testing*, Routledge, London.

Kragh, H (1987) *An Introduction to the Historiography of Science*, Cambridge University Press.

Krueger, R A (1994) *Focus Groups: A practical guide for applied research*, Sage, London.

Kruskal, J B and Wish, M (1978) *Multidimensional Scaling*, Sage, London.

Leinhardt, G (1993) 'Weaving instructional explanations in history', *British Journal of Educational Psychology*, **63** part 1, pp46–74.

Levy, P and Goldstein, H (1984) *Tests in Education: A book of critical reviews*, Academic Press, London.

Litwin, M S (1995) *How to Measure Survey Reliability and Validity*, Sage, London.

Lukes, S (1974) *Power: A radical view*, Macmillan, London.

McGill, I and Beaty, L (1992) *Action Learning: A practitioner's guide*, Kogan Page, London.

Machiavelli, N (1958) *The Prince*, Everyman, London.

McNiff, J (1988) *Action Research: Principles and practice*, Macmillan, London.

Majchrzak, A (1984) *Methods for Policy Research*, Sage, London.

Marsh, C (1988) *Exploring Data: An introduction to data analysis for social scientists*, Polity, Cambridge.

Miles, M B and Huberman, A M C (1994) *Qualitative Data Analysis*, Sage, London.

Miller, P M and Wilson, M J (1983) *A Dictionary of Social Science Methods*, Wiley, Chichester.

Moreland, N, Jawaid, A and Dhillon, J (1998) 'Auditing TESOL: A quality improvement perspective', *TESOL Quarterly*.

Moser, C A and Kalton, G (1971) *Survey Methods in Social Investigation*, Gower, Aldershot.

Mullins, C J (1977) *A Guide to Writing and Publishing in the Social and Behavioural Sciences*, Wiley, Chichester.

Munn, P and Drever, E (1995) *Using Questionnaires in Small-scale Research*, Scottish Council For Research in Education, Edinburgh.

Munroe-Faure, L and Munroe-Faure, M (1992) *Implementing Total Quality Management*, Pitman, London.

Offredy, M (1995) 'Personal narratives of young people working in a caring environment', *Vocational Aspects of Education*, **47** 3, pp309–26.

O'Hanlon, C (ed) (1996) *Professional Development Through Action Research in Educational Settings*, Falmer Press, London.

Olson, J K and Reid, W A (1982) 'Studying innovation in science teaching: The use of repertory grid techniques in developing a research strategy', *European Journal of Science Education*, **4** 2, pp193–201.

Oppenheim, A N (1992) *Questionnaire Design, Interviewing and Attitude Measurement*, Pinter, London.

Osborne, R and Freyberg, P (1985) *Learning in Science: The implications of children's science*, Heinemann, London.

Parkin, F (1971) *Class Inequality and Political Order*, McGibbon & Kee, London.

Patton, M Q (1987) *How to use Qualitative Methods in Evaluation*, Sage, London.

Paulston, R G (1997) 'Mapping visual culture in comparative education discourse', *Compare*, **27** 2, pp117–52.

Peeke, G (1995*) Mission and Change*, Open University Press, Buckingham and Society for Research into Higher Education.

Peters, T J (1987) *Thriving On Chaos*, Random House, London.

Peters, T J and Waterman, R H (1982) *In Search of Excellence: Lessons from America's best companies*, Harper & Row, New York.

Phillips, E M and Pugh, D S (1994) *How to Get a PhD*, Open University Press, Buckingham.

Plewis, I (1997) *Statistics in Education*, Arnold, London.

Pollitt, C (1993) *Managerialism and the Public Services* (2nd edn), Blackwell, Oxford.

Powney, J and Watts, M (1987) *Interviewing in Educational Research*, Routledge, London.

Reason, P (ed) (1994) *Participation in Human Inquiry*, Sage, London.

Ries, J B and Leukefeld, C G (1995) *Applying for Research Funding*, Sage, London.

Sanger, J (1996) *The Compleat Observer? A field research guide to observation*, Falmer Press, London.

Schön, D A (1983) *The Reflective Practitioner*, Basic Books, New York.

Schön, D A (1987) *Educating The Reflective Practitioner*, Jossey-Bass, San Francisco.

Schwandt, T A (1997) *Qualitative Inquiry: A dictionary of terms*, Sage, London.

Scott, J (1991) *Social Network Analysis*, Sage, London.

Scott, J (1990) *A Matter of Record*, Polity, Cambridge.

Siegel, S (1956) *Non-parametric Statistics for the Behavioural Sciences*, McGraw-Hill, Maidenhead.

Simmerman, S J (1994) 'The square wheels of organizational development', *Quality Progress*, **27** 10, pp87–89.

Sinclair, J M and Coulthard, R M (1975) *Towards an Analysis of Discourse*, Oxford University Press.

Stake, R E (1995) *The Art of Case Study Research*, Sage, London.

Stenhouse, L (1975) *An Introduction to Curriculum Research and Development*, Heinemann, London.

Strauss, A and Corbin, J (1989) *Basics of Qualitative Research*, Sage, London.

Stubbs, M (1983) *Discourse Analysis*, Blackwell, Oxford.

Thomas, J (1993) *Doing Critical Ethnography*, Sage, London.

Thomson, A (1996) *Critical Reasoning: A Practical Introduction*, Routledge, London.

Tripp, D (1993) *Critical Incidents in Teaching*, Routledge, London.

Tsoukas, H (ed) (1994) *New Thinking in Organizational Behaviour*, Butterworth-Heinemann, Oxford.

Warren, C E (1987) 'British women and interrupted technological careers: Societal attitudes and patterns of childhood socialization', *International Journal of Lifelong Education*, **6** 2, pp125–51.

Weber, M (1947) *The Theory of Social and Economic Organisation*, Routledge & Kegan Paul, London.

Wilkinson, A and Wilmott, H (1995) *Making Quality Critical*, Routledge, London.

Wright, D B (1997) *Understanding Statistics*, Sage, London.

Wuthnow, R (ed) (1984) *Cultural Analysis*, Routledge & Kegan Paul, London.

Yin, R K (1994) *Case Study Research*, Sage, London.

Yin, R K (1993) *Applications of Case Study Research*, Sage, London.

Zuber-Skerrett, O (ed) (1996) *New Directions in Action Research*, Falmer Press, London.

Zuber-Skerrett, O (1996) 'Introduction: New directions in action research', in Zuber-Skerrett, O (ed) *New Directions in Action Research*, Falmer, London, pp3–9.

Further Reading

Basareb, D J and Root, D K (1992) *The Training Evaluation Process*, Kluwer, Kingston-upon-Thames.

Berry, R (1994) *The Research Project: How to write it*, Routledge, London.

Black, T R (1993) *Evaluating Social Science Research*, Sage, London.

Bolman, L G and Deal, T E (1991) *Reframing Organizations, Artistry, Choice and Leadership*, Jossey-Bass, San Francisco.

Bryman, A and Cramer, D (1990) *Quantitative Data Analysis for Social Scientists*, Routledge, London.

Cassell, C and Symon, G (1994) 'Qualitative research in work contexts', in Cassell, C and Symon, G (eds) (1994), *Qualitative Methods in Organisational Research: A practical guide*, Sage, London, pp1–13.

Clark, P B (1990) *Finding Out in Education: A guide to sources of information*, Longman, Harlow.

Cronbach, L J (1980) *Towards Reform of Program Evaluation*, Jossey-Bass, San Francisco.

Deal, T E and Kennedy, A A (1988) *Corporate Cultures: The rites and rituals of corporate life*, Penguin, Harmondsworth.

Goodson, I F (1992) *Studying Teachers' Lives*, Routledge, London.

Hartley, J F (1994) 'Case studies in organizational research', in Cassell, C and Symon, G (eds), *Qualitative Methods in Organisational Research: A practical guide*, Sage, London, pp208–29.

Holly, M L (1989) *Writing to Grow*, Heinemann, London.

House, E J (1986) *New Directions in Educational Evaluation*, Falmer Press, Lewes.

Jankowicz, A D (1995) *Business Research Projects*, Chapman & Hall, London.

Mason, J (1996) *Qualitative Researching*, Sage, London.

Minichiello, V, Aroni, R, Timewell, E and Alexander, L (1990) *In-depth Interviewing: Researching people*, Longman, Harlow.

Moustakis, C (1994) *Phenomenological Research Methods*, Sage, London.

Orna, E and Stevens, G (1995) *Managing Information for Research*, Open University Press, Buckingham.

Raiborn, C A, Barfield, J T and Kinney, M R (1996) *Managerial Accounting* (2nd edn), West Publishing, St. Paul, MN.

Rossman, M H (1995) *Negotiating Graduate School*, Sage, London.

Rudestrom, K E and Newton, R R (1992) *Surviving Your Dissertation*, Sage, London.

Shaughnessy, J J and Zechmeister, E B (1990) *Research Methods in Psychology*, McGraw-Hill, Maidenhead.

Simpson, M and Tuson, J (1995) *Using Observations in Small-scale Research*, Scottish Council for Research in Education, Edinburgh.

Solomon, R and Winch, C (1994) *Calculating and Computing for Social Science and Arts Students*, Open University Press, Buckingham.

Summers, G F (ed) (1977) *Attitude Measurement*, Kershaw, London.

Tacq, J (1996) *Multivariate Analysis Techniques in Social Science Research*, Sage, London.

Vogt, W P (1993) *Dictionary of Statistics and Methodology*, Sage, London.

Willcox, B (1992) *Time-constrained Evaluation*, Routledge, London.

Winter, R (1987) *Action Research and the Nature of Social Inquiry*, Gower Publications, Aldershot.

Index

References in italic indicate figures or tables.

abstracting publications 89
abstraction levels of research
    questions 10–12
abstracts 92, 148
access to data 2, 14–15, 22, 86
'accounts' method 54–5
action research 34–5, 113–14, 128–9,
    129
active reading 90–92
advocacy-adversary evaluation 126
AIM (Author's Intended Message)
    90–93
aims of book 1–4
aims of research, reviewing 131
archives *see* libraries
articles in journals, citing 98
Asher, M 117, *117*, 121
Atkinson, P 52
attitude measurement 48–9
authors, comparing 94–5
Author's Intended Message (AIM)
    90–93

Bennett, R 103
bibliographies
    constructing own 86–8, 97–100
    using existing 89, 92
bids for funding 19, 20–24
biographical research 37–8, 54–5
Bolman, L G 106, 107
book publication 152–3
books, citing 97–8
borrowing rights 86
briefings, overseas research 26
British Education Index Line 141–2
budgets 21–3

Caldwell, B J 125
calendars 7
canvassed research 20
career paths 37–8, 77
case studies 36
Cassell, C 113
catalogues, library 87
categorisation methods 74–5
citation methods 3, 96–100
'client' concept 118
cluster analysis 69
cluster sampling 44
coding 58, 59–61, 72
    questionnaires 47–8
collaborators 13
commissioned research 19
communication facilities, overseas
    research 26–7
computer uses 3, 136–43
    construction of reports 142
    data analysis 15, 27, 137–41, *139*,
        140
    getting information 141–2
conclusions of reports 92, 101, 149–50
concurrent validity 42
conference presentations 152
consumer trials 120–21
content analysis 53–4, 72–4
contingency table analysis 66, *66*
contributions in books, citing 98–9
Cook, S 122
correlational research 33
correlations 64–6, 71
costings 21–3
critical ethnography 36
critical incident methods 37–8, 54

critical path analysis 6–7, *8*
cross-sectional studies 34
cultural perspective 109–10
customer needs research 117–21, *120*

Dale, B G 116
data analysis 2–3, 58–79, 149
　coding 58, 59–61
　initial plans 15–16, 48
　presentation 58–9
　qualitative 72–9, *78*
　quantitative 61–71, *62, 65, 66, 68, 69*
data collection 2, 14–15, 39, 40–57
　methods 45–56
　sampling 44–5
　validity and reliability 41–5
Deal, T E 106, 107
decision-oriented evaluation 126
'deliberate creation' aspect of
　　organizations 104–5
Delphi technique 50
descriptive statistics 61
developmental methods 34
*Diagnostic Approach to Organizational
　Behaviour* 112
diaries 54
difference, tests of 64
discourse analysis 78
discursive practice 104, 134
discriminant analysis 70
'discussion' sections 149–50
dissertations indexes 88–9, 145

'ease of use' factors 44
emic perspective 36
empirical evidence 9
equipment 22, 57
Ericsson, K A 55
ethical issues 2, 14, 24–5, 133
ethnographic methods 35, 76–7
ethnomethodological paradigms 31
etic perspective 36
evaluation of research 3, 123, 124–8, *124*
evaluation research method 36
ex post facto research 34

experimental research 32–3
expert panels 42
explanatory evaluation 126
exploratory data analysis 68–9, *69*

face validity 42
factor analysis 42, 70
Fetterman, D M 35–6
field journals 135
Fitz-Gibbon, C T 118
fixed costs 23
focus groups 50–51, 121
follow-up research 3–4, 154
formative evaluation 125
Fuller, R 129
funding 2, 17–27
　allocation criteria 20, 23–4
　bids 20–23
　sources 18–19
　types 19–20

Garvin, D A 129–30
general funding agencies 18–19
generic review capabilities 84–5
goal-free evaluation 126
'goal-oriented' aspect of
　　organizations 105–6
goal-oriented evaluation 126
Gordon, Judith 112, *113*
government publications, citing 99
grants *see* funding
grounded v. traditional theory 29
group interviews 50–51, 121

Hammersley, M 52
Harvard system 96–7
Hatch, J A 77
Hawthorne effect 33
Herman, J L 126–7
historical research 36–7, 53, 120–21
Hitchcock, G 37
'house of quality' 121, *122*
Hughes, A 37
'human resource' perspective 110–12

ideational perspective 110
implications of research 133

in house publication 152
inferential statistics 61–2, 64–6, *65*, *66*
internal process control 122
internal validity 42
Internet 141
interventionist methodologies 31
'Interview about Instances' 50
interviews 49–51
introductions to reports 148

journal publication 152, 153
journals, citing articles from 98

Kanji, G K 117, *117*, 121
Krueger, R A 121

language skills 27
learning organizations 129–30
libraries 14, 22, 29–30, 53, 85–6
    catalogues 87
life history approach 37–8, 77
literature reviews 3, 80–101, 148–9
    bibliographies/references 96–100
    definition and purpose 81–4
    starting 85–9
    techniques and skills 84–5, 90–96

major evaluation 125
management cycle of activity 122–3,
    123
management principles (Peters) 111
market research 36, 120–21
materialist perspective 110
methodologies 2, 28–39, 113–14
    paradigms 30–31
    qualitative/quantitative 31–8
    reviewing 131–2
Miller, P M 41, 43
mimeographs, citing 99–100
minor evaluation 125
monitoring 123–4, *124*
Morris, L L 118
multidimensional scaling 71
multilevel modelling 72

needs identification 117–21
network methods 75–6

nominal data 62
non-interventionist methods 31
non-ratio data 63
normal distribution curve 63–4
note making 93–4
null hypotheses 7–8

'objective-oriented' aspect of
    organizations 105–6
objectivist paradigms 30
observation methods 51–2
one-tailed tests 67
'openness' ethic 25
ordinal data 62
organization research 3, 102–14
    characteristics 106–7
    definition 103–6
    perspectives 107–12
    topics and methods 112–14, *113*
originality 21, 28–30, 147
overseas research 2, 25–7

page referencing 94
paradigms 29, 30–31
part funding 18
path analysis 71
Patton, M Q 127
'people' aspect of organizations
    103–4
'perspectives' of organizational
    research 107–12
PERT analysis 6–7
Petch, A 129
Peters, T J 110, 111
pilot studies 42
plagiarism 94
planning 2, 5–16, 38–9
    funding bids 20–23
    overseas research 26
    project phases 5–7, *8*
    research questions 7–13
Plunkett, D 116
policy research 36–7
political perspective 108–9
positivist paradigms 30, 31
'power' perspective 108
predictive validity 42

primary sources 53
principal components analysis 70
prompt questions 50
protocol analysis 55
publication of reports 3, 152–4

QFD *see* quality function
    deployment
qualitative data analysis 15, 59, 72–9,
    78
  coding 61, 72
  computer packages 139–41, *140*
qualitative methodologies 31–2,
    35–8, 120–21
  evaluation 127–8
quality function deployment (QFD)
    121, 122
quality improvement 3, 115–29
  action research 128–9, *128*
  customer needs 117–21, *120*
  definition 116–17, *117*
  evaluation/monitoring 124–9, *124*
  internal control 122–4, *123*
quantitative data analysis 15, 58–9,
    61–72
  coding 59–60
  complex analysis 68–72, *69*
  computer packages 137–9, *139*
  simple analysis 61–8, *62*, *65*, *66*
quantitative methodologies 31–5
  evaluation 127
quantity data 62
questionnaires 45–9
quotations 94, 95, 96–7

random sampling 44
ratio data 63
reading rights 86
reading techniques 90–93
realist paradigms 30
record keeping 25
references, citing 3, 96–100
reflecting on research 13, 131–5
regional funding organizations 18
regression methods 71
reliability 43, 52
repertory grid methods 56

report preparation 3, 22, 144–54
  computer uses 142–3
  originality 147
  starting 145–7
  structure 147–50
'research culture' 154
research questions 7–13, 149
resource issues *see* funding
'respect for persons' ethic 24
'respect for truth' ethic 25
responsive evaluation 126
responsive research 19–20
results, reviewing 132–3
reviews *see* reflecting on research

sampling 44–5, 132
scheduling 6–7, *8*
Schwandt, T A 104, 134
Scott, J 53
secondary market research 121
secondary sources 53
semantic net systems 77, *78*
serial reading 87
significance tests 67
Simon, H A 55
snowballing 87
sociometry 56
specialist funding foundations 18
Spinks, J M 125
'split-result' reliability 43
staff costings 21–2
stakeholders 118–19
standard deviation 63–4
statistical sources 53
stem and leaf plots 69, *69*
stratified sampling 44, 118
structural perspective 107–8
subheadings 93
summative evaluation 125
survey methods 34
Symons, G 113

task lists 6
test-retest method 43
testing methods 55–6
tests, statistical 64–6, *65*, *66*
textual analysis 53

theory and originality 28, 29–30
theses, citing 99
theses indexes 88–9, 145
'thick description' method 54–5
time management 5–6
timescales, reviewing 132
titles of books/reports 91–2, 148
total quality management (TQM)
    116–17, *117*
tracer studies 38
track records 20–21
traditional v. grounded theory 29
triangulation 42–3
two-tailed tests 67

USA, funding sources 18

utilization-oriented research 126

validity 41–3, 52
value judgements 9
variability within samples 63
variable costs 23
viva voces 151–2

Waterman, R H 111
whole funding 18
Wilson, M J 41, 43
Wisniewski, R 77
working hypotheses 9

Zuber-Skerrett, O 129